6/06

DAT

Best Practices
in Adult Learning

Best Practices
in Adult Learning

Lee Bash
Averett University

EDITOR

Anker Publishing Company, Inc.
Bolton, Massachusetts

Best Practices in Adult Learning

ISBN 1-882982-78-9

Composition by Lyn Rodger, Deerfoot Studios
Cover design by Dutton & Sherman Design

Anker Publishing Company, Inc.
563 Main Street
P.O. Box 249
Bolton, MA 01740-0249 USA

www.ankerpub.com

Library of Congress Cataloging-in-Publication Data

Best practices in adult learning / Lee Bash, editor.
    p. cm.
Includes bibliographical references and index.
  ISBN 1-882982-78-9
  1. Adult education. I. Bash, Lee, 1941–

LC5215.B49 2005
374—dc22

                                                      2004026505

About the Authors

The Editor

Lee Bash is dean of graduate and professional studies at Averett University, a program with four regional centers and more than 25 satellite sites serving more than two-thirds of the school's total enrollment. Since the publication of his previous book, *Adult Learners in the Academy* (Anker, 2003), he has consulted and presented on the unique and special issues associated with adult learners. He was recently asked by the American Council on Education to serve as resident scholar for 2004–2005 on a task force focusing on the topic of adult learners in 21st-century higher education.

The Contributors

Linda Anderson holds a bachelor's degree in social work, a master's degree in human ecology, and a second master's degree in education. Her work background includes teaching at all age levels and social work for the Department of Social Services. As a volunteer, she has worked with homeless shelters, community mental health, foster/respite care for medically fragile children, and as a learning partner for at-risk children in elementary schools.

Patricia R. Brewer has developed and administered programs in adult higher education since 1980. She holds an Ed.D. in adult and continuing education from Teachers College Columbia University and has served as president of the Adult Higher Education Alliance. She currently serves in a full-time capacity at Walden University, where she works with the adult education and community college leadership programs.

Sue Grunau received a bachelor's degree in education from Baldwin-Wallace College and a master's degree in education with a specialization in community agency counseling from Cleveland State University. She has worked in a variety of settings including mental health agencies, industry, and institutions of higher education. Her most recent employment with the University of Michigan and Baldwin-Wallace College has focused on advising adult students who are returning to school to complete their formal education.

Iris H. Kelsen has been affiliated with Wilmington College since 1988 and has been associate vice president for academic affairs and dean of the Cincinnati Branches since 1997. She has more than 20 years of increasing responsibility in higher education academic administration with a primary focus on adult learners, including proven success in designing and implementing curriculum and establishing and administering branch campuses. She has an MBA in accounting from Case Western Reserve University.

Lawrence T. Lesick is associate vice president for enrollment management at Widener University. He has more than 20 years of experience in enrollment management, including the areas of admission and recruitment, financial aid and student accounts, integrated marketing, publications, academic records, student one-stop service center, retention, and institutional research. He has published and made presentations on such topics as admission and financial aid, business process redesign, and American religious history. He received a Ph.D. in religion from Vanderbilt University in 1979.

Charlene L. Martin has been dean of continuing education at Assumption College since 1998 and has more than 20 years of experience in the field of continuing higher education. She received her Ed.D. at the University of Massachusetts–Amherst in educational policy, research, and administration. She has published and presented her research on older adult learners and learning in retirement institutes and has received several awards for her work with the Worcester Institute for Senior Education. Most recently, she was awarded the William C. Hine Distinguished Service Award from Alpha Sigma Lambda. In 2003, Dr. Martin completed a three-year term on the board of directors of the Association for Continuing Higher Education.

Margie Martyn recently served as the assistant dean of lifelong learning at Baldwin-Wallace College where she designed and implemented a hybrid distance learning model. The model, which utilizes various computer-mediated communication components, has been published in a recent issue of *Educause Quarterly*. Her Ph.D. is from the University of Akron, where her doctoral research focused on the impact of online threaded discussion in both face-to-face and online courses. She has presented on her research in computer-mediated communication at several conferences.

Stuart Noble-Goodman received his bachelor's degree in English from the University of California–Berkeley, and has worked in the U.S. Senate and the private sector. He earned his doctorate in English at Duke University in 1996. He was then appointed director of graduate teacher education programs at North Carolina State University, where he served until taking a position in the English department at Benedictine University. While at Benedictine, he served as director of the writing and honors programs. In 1999, he moved to the University of Redlands as associate dean of Whitehead College. In 2003, he was appointed interim dean of the School of Business at the University of Redlands.

Walter Pearson has been associate dean for academic affairs and director of the Division of Adult Learning at Simpson College for 10 years. He has provided leadership and service to adult learners throughout his professional career. His award-winning program at Simpson College has achieved national attention with its innovations balanced by recognition as a benchmark among adult learner programs.

Bruce Pietrykowski holds a doctorate in economics from the New School for Social Research and is associate professor of economics in the Department of Social Sciences at the University of Michigan–Dearborn (UM–Dearborn). He was director of the distance learning program in the College of Arts, Sciences, and Letters at UM–Dearborn from 1996 to 2001 where he also served as associate dean. In addition to teaching and conducting research in economics, he currently directs the Center for the Study of Automotive Heritage at UM–Dearborn. He also serves on the editorial boards of the *Review of Radical Political Economics* (Sage) and the *Review of Social Economy* (Routledge). His research on topics in adult education and instructional technology is published in *Adult Education Quarterly* and the *Journal of Economic Issues.*

Karen I. Rhoda is director of The University of Toledo's Division of Distance Learning and has built this organization into the successful enterprise it is today. She earned her Ph.D. from The University of Toledo. She chairs the provost's Distance Learning Advisory Committee, serves on Ohio Learning Network's Academic Outreach and Distance and eLearning Futures Task Force Committees, and on the United States Distance Learning Association's (USDLA) Advisory Board. She was nominated to the USDLA in 2002 for outstanding leadership in distance learning. She has been a presenter at numerous state, regional, national, and international conferences.

W. Hubbard Segur is a professor in the School of Business at the University of Redlands. He received his Ph.D. from the University of California–Davis and has taught for more than 20 years in the field of economics. He has initiated and collaborated on adjunct faculty mentoring, development, and empowerment since 1991. He has developed a variety of best practices workshops which reach back to Gappa and Leslie's research and findings in *The Invisible Faculty* (Jossey-Bass, 1993).

Sean Warner is a native of the United Kingdom. He did his undergraduate studies in classical Semitic languages in Ireland at Trinity College and later received his Ph.D. in ancient near eastern history from Hebrew Union College. He has been involved in adult higher education for a number of years in both the United Kingdom and the United States. He is currently dean of adult and professional studies at Friends University.

Table of Contents

Part IV: Technological Applications

Part V: Adult Learning Includes Senior Learners

Preface

Overview

When I first envisioned this book, I wanted to offer something to balance and reinforce the material covered in its predecessor, *Adult Learners in the Academy* (2003). For that book, the intended audience extended beyond practitioners in adult learning to include faculty and administrators who, I assumed, were less familiar with the phenomenon of adult learners. At the same time, I hoped they would be interested to learn how valuable adult learners are as a distinct population. An additional objective was for the book to serve as a prototype by providing insights and examples for the academy. It has long been my contention that adult learner programs, with their longstanding history of surviving under extraordinary challenges, serve as a model for the 21st-century academy. I hoped that readers were looking for insights and foundations for this dynamic population of students.

Feedback from *Adult Learners in the Academy* confirmed that many professionals in adult learning had shared the book with their faculty and administrators less familiar with adult learners. I also heard that many colleagues in continuing education were looking for more fundamental, hands-on guidance and applications. Consequently, the purpose of this book is to share with fellow adult educators some of the best practices I have encountered or learned about in my own pursuit of this topic.

A quick perusal of the contents of this book will reveal that the contributors represent a wide range of practitioners—geographically and academically. There is literally a coast-to-coast dimension among the authors. In addition, every type of institution is represented here. The expertise of the contributors is exceptional. If you gain as much from reading this book as I did assembling the material, it should serve you particularly well—I have already accessed these handy chapters on more than one occasion to glean useful applications in my everyday experience.

When I speak at various institutions and conferences, I am always struck by the diversity of descriptions offered to explain what it is we do in "continuing education." I've also noticed how dynamic and volatile a topic we and the adult students we serve appear to be for faculty and administrators on many campuses. At some schools, it seems that discussions about various aspects of adult learning are much like politics or religion—to be approached with delicacy and reserve.

Though I had written about marginalization of adult degree completion programs in *Adult Learners in the Academy,* I never imagined I would encounter the degree of resistance and animosity aimed at this population that I have recently experienced at some institutions. On some campuses, attitudes and behaviors concerning adult learners appear to be extremely negative and frenetic, though disorganized. On the other hand, some schools have made exceptional efforts to inculcate adult learners into their identity and culture. In other words, the academy appears to reflect a growing dichotomy when it comes to adult learners, with strong convictions expressed on either side. All this has helped convince me that the need for identifying best practices is more critical than ever, especially as the stakes among competitors continue to rise.

Introduction

In 2002, I was dean of lifelong learning at Baldwin-Wallace College when it was selected to participate in a pilot project as one of approximately 20 schools chosen by the Council for Adult and Experiential Learning (CAEL). The project's objective was to identify the characteristics that CAEL believed were consistent with Adult Learning Focused Institutions (ALFI). Initially, I was anxious for our program to be selected (there were more than 100 applicants) simply because of the prestige associated with the selection process and the inherent benefits I was certain the program would accrue. However, as the year progressed and we became more involved with the developing stages of the pilot, I found myself fascinated with observing commonalities, strengths, and distinguishing features of what proved to be a fairly diverse group of adult programs.

Like many of my colleagues—directors and deans of adult programs that had been carefully selected to participate in this pilot—I had anticipated significant benefits associated with being officially designated as an ALFI program. But when we administrators were finally able to gather together to share our experiences and make some sense out of them, many of us were disappointed to learn that our expectations did not necessarily align with CAEL's objectives for the ALFI project. To their credit, CAEL never implied that the ALFI designation certified or accredited any of the participating institutions, nor was that ever their intention. Nonetheless, I observed that many of the participating programs were seeking such validation or confirmation along with clear criteria to reinforce that decision—balanced by the need to determine their strengths and weaknesses. I believe that it will only be a matter of time before some educational organization—probably affiliated with adult learning—will provide the sort of accreditation that already exists on many college campuses associated with professional programs in business, music, medicine, and other disciplines.

The need to improve our programs and compare them with benchmarks is powerful. The level of competition for adult learners has become dramatic. These aspects have helped bring greater attention to best practices and increase interest among many administrators who might have previously ignored the adult learner population. As Freeman (2003) noted,

> In the world of continuing higher education, we are being asked more than ever before to justify the quality of our programs, not only in terms of fiscal strength and revenue generation, but also in terms of instructional quality and responsiveness to the needs of learners and the marketplace. (p. 23)

I've encountered this phenomenon when I've served as a consultant-evaluator for various adult programs throughout the country. Indeed, many of the lessons learned offered at the end of this preface are derived from experiences I've had with these diverse institutions. The whole notion of best practices seems to resonate for adult programs and their institutions in a way that might not have seemed conceivable a few short years ago.

Outline of the Book

Despite some misconceptions likely to be held by those faculty and administrators who do not work directly with the adult learner population, adult learning programs have a much greater level of complexity and depth than may be apparent. For many administrators, these programs might be reduced to issues of revenue or enrollment generation, but successful models comprise many segments—each of which must function at the optimum if the program is going to flourish. This book is likewise segmented to better capture many of the more critical elements associated with outstanding programs.

Part I: Laying the Foundation for Best Practices is designed to serve as a primer for addressing fundamental aspects of any program. This segment is devoted to issues that relate to vision. Each chapter answers the question, "What do I want my program to contain or deliver?" While these chapters may tend to be a bit more abstract than the remainder of the book, they cover essential issues to help define and optimize adult learning programs. For instance, Chapter 1, Applications of Multiple Intelligences for Adult Learners, answers that question with a response that reflects sensitivity to the diverse needs of individual adult learners. It highlights recent advances in the field of multiple intelligences—first introduced by the famous learning psychologist Howard Gardner—as they are now beginning to be applied to adult learners. Readers whose programs do not currently address this topic will want to read it carefully in consideration of applications to be shared with their faculty and students.

If your answer to the question relies heavily on a cohort model—where groups of students progress through their coursework in lockstep fashion—Chapter 2, Bridging the Gap: Improving Graduation Rates in a Degree Completion Program, will hold special interest for you. In recent years, adult programs that utilize cohorts as their delivery method often encounter problems relating to graduation that may be more pronounced than with less structured programs, where students are able to pick and choose courses and sequences. Although this model produces some distinctive advantages, it also offers some unique challenges. Chapter 2 addresses many useful ideas regarding solutions and alternatives that one program has identified when confronting one of the most characteristic of those challenges.

On the other hand, if the answer to the question is somewhat unclear to you—if you are looking for some fundamentals to help determine just exactly what options your program will reflect—Chapter 3, Program Planning and Review in Adult Higher Education: Using Program Models Effectively, addresses the very essence of laying foundations as it examines systematic program planning and then provides models from one of the nation's leading authorities. Even if your program is already well defined, you will want to review this chapter to ensure nothing has been overlooked.

If Part I is a bit abstract, **Part II: Defining Moments in Adult Learner Programs** is just the opposite with a nuts-and-bolts, hands-on set of applications that are designed to strengthen your daily practices and options. If there is one aspect of adult learning programs that has emerged as more essential than any other in defining successful programs, it is the topic of strategic partnerships. Chapter 4, Strategic Partnerships: Successfully Managing Collaborative Ventures in Adult Education, provides guidelines and recommendations derived from the author's experiences with a series of longstanding and highly successful partnerships among and between schools and corporations. This is a topic that appears to have special interest for the 21st-century academy, particularly adult learner programs.

Although a natural tension may exist between those who work in admissions (since they are typically accountable for producing ever-increasing numbers) and those who work on the academic side (since they are likely to want these students to possess the qualities that will ensure their success), Chapter 5, Recruiting and Admitting Adult Learners: They're Not Just Older—They're Different, demonstrates that there is a way to strike a good balance and achieve a win/win relationship with these sometimes competing perspectives. The chapter contains recommendations for recruiting and admitting adult learners—the first essential component of enrollment management. The authors indicate how decisions for adult learners often play a critical role in the success of a program.

Of course, once you admit good students, an equal challenge relates to their retention, which provides a balance for the overall enrollment perspective. Research has indicated that strong advising may be the most essential and critical factor relating to retention for adult learners. Chapter 6, Adult Learner Advising: The Vital Link, provides a number of successful applications taken from a diverse set of schools and programs.

Chapter 7, The Introductory Transformation Course for Adult Learners: Critical and Essential, looks at what many successful programs consider to be a critical retention factor: the introductory course designed for adult learners. Not simply an advanced version of College 101, this essential course often determines both the success of the student and the ability of the program to provide a stable foundation for retention. As such, this type of course often serves as a transformation for adult learners, particularly if they have been away from the classroom for an extended period.

Part III: Faculty Development: A Key to Instructional Effectiveness emphasizes the importance of faculty development for the health and vitality of successful adult programs. There are simply too many aspects of adult learning that are unique and distinctive—where the job can't be done with cookie-cutter solutions used in traditional classrooms. The part's two chapters—Chapter 8, Adjunct Faculty Training, and Chapter 9,

Assuring Instructional Effectiveness—address different aspects of faculty development and will provide readers with useful information from which to develop their own faculty development programs.

It would be impossible to write about best practices in adult learning without referencing technology. There are many books that are devoted exclusively to the topic of **Part IV: Technological Applications,** so the two chapters that are presented here may seem a bit sparse. However, each chapter is distinctive and full of immediate applications. Furthermore, these chapters are written in straightforward, easy-to-understand language with no jargon or complex descriptions that might otherwise restrict or inhibit readers. Chapter 10, The Role of Distance Education in Enhancing Accessibility for Adult Learners, was written by an extremely successful administrator whose distance learning program has experienced phenomenal growth in a short period of time. Since this program defines "success" by any standard you may select, this is clearly a chapter you will want to take careful note of, since it deals with enhancing accessibility for adult learners through the use of distance learning.

The use and applications of computers has risen so rapidly in education that it is sometimes hard to know which classroom or pedagogical practices are appropriate. This is an area where good research to support best practices is especially helpful, and building a foundation for research is the focus of Chapter 11, Computer-Mediated Communication: A Quest for Quality.

Part V: Adult Learning Includes Senior Learners deserves consideration even if some of your programs do not necessarily make any special provisions for this select population. As the fastest growing demographic in America today, senior learners will make their presence felt on college campuses in many new ways as more schools recognize their importance on many levels. Chapter 12, Meeting the Needs of Older Adult Learners: The Development of a Learning in Retirement Institute, investigates a successful model program and provides philosophical support to help you work with this population.

Lessons Learned

Each chapter includes a list of lessons learned to help readers replicate the authors' successes and avoid their blunders. These lessons are typically located at the end of each chapter.

The following are lessons which I gleaned from among the contributors or from observations and assessments I made during speaking engagements and consultative activities.

Proper Structure Is Essential

If the continuing education unit is designed with various components reporting to different individuals, the system will not function at its best—even if everyone works well together. If there are different components (one portion responsible for admissions with another accountable for curricular delivery, for instance), they often work at cross purposes. The best systems use a structure where one leader is responsible for everyone in the unit.

Mission Statements and Leadership Vision Must Align

If the unit is incompatible with the mission of the institution or vision of the leadership, systemic problems will inevitably follow. This may seem obvious, but many programs encounter more internal challenges and obstacles than external. Without the right support system (starting at the very top), adult learner programs are vulnerable and can be jeopardized. One of the first elements I look for in this regard is a mission statement for the unit to compare with its institution's mission statement. If these don't align, other challenges will be evident as well. In this same regard, recent experiences reveal that even outstanding adult learner programs can be dismantled when the vision of new leadership doesn't value them.

The Best Adult Learner Programs Can Never Rest on Their Laurels

If your program isn't already planning for its next change, you're in trouble. The 21st-century academy is dominated by change. Successful competition means being able to anticipate changes and stay near the front of the parade. It means being able to reinvent your program and make wise, well-informed decisions. It means being open to all options and seeing opportunities everywhere. But the best characteristic I've encountered has been a willingness to seek constructive criticism in order to improve. This process can be accomplished in any number of ways, from hiring a consultant to self-assessment. Through the use of formative assessment, any program can continue to improve.

Successful Adult Learner Programs Are Learner-Centered and Entrepreneurial

Adult learners are often outspoken and direct in articulating their needs and expectations. Best practices reflect sensitivity to whatever issues might arise as a result of such feedback. Leadership in these areas often takes this process one step further by anticipating these needs and creating responses that produce direct pathways to the programs and unique features that distinguish them from everyone else.

References

Bash, L. (2003). *Adult learners in the academy.* Bolton, MA: Anker.

Freeman, M. (2003, Winter). Assessing and evaluating continuing education programs: Why and how? *Journal of Continuing Higher Education, 51*(1), 23–30.

Part I

Laying the Foundation for Best Practices

1

Applications of Multiple Intelligences for Adult Learners

Linda Anderson

The last 20 years have brought many changes in the ways that we look at education, impacting everyone from young children to adults. The tremendous expansion of knowledge about the brain and how people learn has empowered us to look differently at how we understand intelligence, provide learning experiences, and demonstrate accomplished knowledge.

For many years educators believed that human learning and behavior came only as a result of outside stimuli. They mistakenly believed that if the good students continued to be encouraged and rewarded, surely their learning would continue on a successful path. On the other side, punishment was the best answer to coerce students into leaving poor learning behaviors behind and embracing more positive and appropriate learning behaviors. At the heart of this thinking was that the teacher was in control of all learning. The teacher was the director! Today we are more likely to view the teacher as the facilitator, not the director, of a learning environment.

Learning is instead, from birth, an internal and biologically driven need to know for survival. All one has to do is to spend some time in a room full of two-year-olds to know that this internal drive to explore and learn is very strong. What is unfortunate is that so many people lose this drive as they progress through inappropriate learning environments that emphasize only one or two ways of learning, problem solving, or applications of knowledge.

My Learning Revolution

I am truly amazed at what I thought I knew when I graduated from college and began teaching, compared to what I now believe and know about working in a learning environment. The cognitive revolution, based on brain research, has forever changed my beliefs. It really wasn't until long after I got my first master's degree that it began to dawn on me that I had found much of what was, for years, a void or gap in my teaching. In my early years of teaching, I always had a gut feeling that there was something missing and that I was either not reaching some of my students or that they simply were not "learners."

In recent years I began to change the focus of my own studies and started looking more carefully at how students absorb, process, and expand their own learning. These observations led to research that led me to believe that all students were intelligent in some way, certainly on different levels, but that they all had the capacity to learn. It also created a new view of learning that emphasized student-initiated application of knowledge in a learning environment based on problem solving. Because I teach multiple classes at the community college level, I see mostly adult students who have returned to school for various reasons. Perhaps a job has forced them to expand their education, or they are being retrained because of a job loss, or they just want a better-paying job, or they have finally found the courage to pursue a dream. Many of them are reluctant learners, or learners who have been unsuccessful in their past educational experiences. I questioned why these students were unsuccessful, since I was convinced they had the capacity to learn.

The Multiple Intelligence Solution

This search for a deeper understanding of the adult learner led me to the work of Howard Gardner of Harvard University, and his theory about multiple intelligences. His work was the final piece in my search for greater understanding of the phenomenon of the adult learner. Gardner challenges our thinking about intelligence. He believes that intelligence is not fixed, but rather can be developed and demonstrated in many ways. He questions the traditional views that we can test in traditional ways and thus identify the intelligence of people. According to Gardner (1993), what we are really testing is the potential for success in only two areas: linguistics and logical or mathematical intelligence. Even within these two areas, we rarely look at how a student can use information and knowledge.

For many years, I have viewed students as puzzles—often to themselves and to their teachers. It is only after we, as partners with the students, gather multiple pieces of their puzzle that we can get a sense of who they are, what their potential might be, and how they use learning to solve problems. For Gardner, this ability to solve problems, particularly within one's own culture, community, or society, is the real center of intelligence. Gardner suggests that intelligence is not a measurable score or number and cannot be used to define someone's probability for success.

Unfortunately, many educators have a distorted view of the intelligence of a student—based only on what he or she can produce according to a set of expectations and demonstrations that the teacher has set. This tends to create a false view of a student's real intelligence. It provides an easy way to determine a grade, but it does not tell us how to make the information useful and applicable for them and how they might use it to expand their base of "knowing" as they move through life. Indeed, the real measure of success in education may be how well students apply learning. How do they make it relevant and meaningful, or use it to solve problems within the context of the values of their culture?

Gardner (1983, 1993) refers to eight different types of intelligences: linguistic, logical/mathematical, spatial, bodily/kinesthetic, musical, interpersonal, intrapersonal, and naturalist (see Figure 1.1). All students have some portion of each one of the eight intelligences. These are often demonstrated in different ways, according to the context or situations in which people find themselves. However, most individuals have a higher level of ability in one or two of the intelligences.

Perhaps what's most important is that we can all develop these intelligences for ourselves, especially in certain contexts. Many individuals are very intelligent in areas that are less acceptable in the classroom and are therefore incorrectly labeled. For example, dyslexic students are frequently very strong in visual/spatial intelligence, and students who are labeled hyperactive are often very strong in bodily/kinesthetic intelligence. Some students with lower logical/mathematical or verbal/linguistic skills are accomplished in interpersonal skills and end up in important supervisory positions, at times overseeing those with higher mathematical and linguistic skills.

FIGURE 1.1

The Eight Multiple Intelligences

Linguistic
Loves playing with words, reading, listening, and writing

Logical/Mathematical
Loves patterns, reasoning, deducting, calculating, and hypothesizing

Spatial
Likes to learn visually, represents ideas in projects or by drawing or sketching or other art forms

Bodily/Kinesthetic
Strong hand-eye coordination, fluid body movements, loves learning through body activities

Musical
Loves rhythm, tones, instruments, singing, and listening to music

Interpersonal
Is very aware of others and their feelings, loves interacting and helping others

Intrapersonal
Loves self-reflection, setting goals, being self-disciplined

Naturalist
Loves nature, animals, the order and patterns of plant life and ecological issues

This is a significant change in how instructors view the learning potential of their students. Once this concept is integrated, it can become one of the most empowering tools that professors can utilize to make a class more meaningful and successful for many different types of adult learners.

Gardner (1991) often refers to the individualization of education engendered by his theory. The theory recognizes the differences in learning, appreciates the varying strengths of learners, and provides an environment of multiple learning perspectives. It looks at how a student might apply what he or she knows and understands in different ways. As a first step in that direction, I like to help students think about their own multiple intelligences. I have them write the eight intelligences on paper and then think about what they most like to do, how they interact with other people, how they spend their leisure time, and how they study. I have them identify what helps them learn new information best, what their career plans are, and why they chose that career. Then I ask them to select one thing: If they could do anything they wanted to do for one whole day, what would it be? After this introspective exercise, I have them place themselves into the circles of intelligences, with a one being most favored and a four being least favored.

The Myers-Briggs Type Indicator is used in some classes to help students understand themselves and their gifts. Additionally, Silver, Strong, and Perini's (2000) book, *So Each May Learn,* contains a useful multiple intelligence indicator tool that is followed by a learning style inventory. When used together, these two measures are powerful assessment tools to assist students in understanding their own learning. For the first class session, I often use a worksheet that I created to help students see how multiple intelligences differ when compared with their fellow students. I also encourage them to remember the students who have different stronger intelligences or combinations of intelligences, since they may want to pair up with those students to do a project assignment for class. This worksheet has students interview other students to see where they might fit in the multiple intelligences. This helps them appreciate the differences in their classmates and see how different intelligences can be complementary to each other.

Applications

Teachers have to apply what students have discovered about themselves and their own learning. I often use a technique that I call *cognitive webbing* (Figure 1.2). In the center I put the learning topic that we are covering. In my class planning I try to incorporate all the intelligences in my ideas for presenting the information. When we have covered the material, I put the learning topic on the board in class and create circles for all of the multiple intelligences. Using this diagram, I then ask the students to demonstrate what they have learned. I am always amazed at how students, who have begun the journey of understanding their own learning, can develop such creative ideas for demonstration. Of course, there are still some learners who want to take a more conventional test so I offer two choices, multiple-choice or essay tests.

Cognitive Webbing

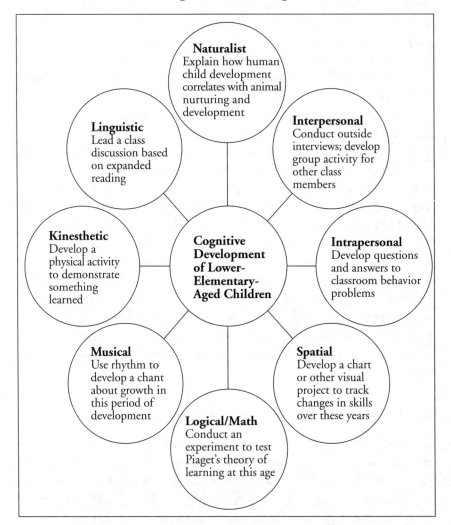

In another application, a history instructor at my college (Northwestern Michigan College, a community college) encourages students to choose from a list of ways to learn new material and to share their choice with the class. He suggests that students whose major intelligence is bodily/kinesthetic perform and/or create dramas about history, play "Great Moments from the Past" charades, or explore dances from history. For students whose strengths are more intrapersonal, he offers options that might include keeping a journal of questions about a student's personal life that might be better understood from a historical perspective. He also presents students with a chance to write an essay concerning past mistakes that they would not repeat or imagine people from the past giving advice to people today. For the students who are more musical, he has them analyze history through the music of various periods, create a historical rap, or demonstrate some music from past histories. He offers ideas for each of the intelligences and then brainstorms with the students concerning what they might do if they are having trouble determining what might work best for them.

A communication instructor who teaches remedial English for community college students does some innovative things to help accommodate both adult and traditional learners who are struggling to learn grammar skills or writing skills. She asks students to create songs or visual illustrations and design games and stories as ways to teach grammar rules and syntax. She also allows students to make up dances for various parts of speech, or play parts of a sentence charade. Sometimes she has students think about themselves in a story and then write or talk about how they would have approached and solved a problem differently than the characters in the story.

The point of these exercises is to emphasize that once teachers begin to appreciate multiple intelligences, they begin to see how learning can take on new directions and how each student becomes intelligent in his or her own way. When you look at people around you who are successful at solving problems related to themselves or the well-being of a community or culture, then you also see high levels of varying intelligences. With this insight comes the ability to provide a new type of product, whether real or service-related. This also helps reinforce how a community survives and is productive due to the contributions of many people.

Lessons Learned

This evolutionary journey in teaching adult learners by using multiple intelligences has been a challenge. I spend more time connecting with students and their multiple intelligences. I also spend more time preparing
for classes so that I can make use of the intelligences that my students
bring. Most significantly, I have had to let go of some old ways of presenting information and let the students design and direct more of their own
learning. The rewards are well worth the journey. Learning for my students has become more exciting, more internalized, and more useful to
them as they continue in the academic world.

References

Gardner, H. (1983). *Frames of mind: The theory of multiple intelligences.*
New York, NY: Basic Books.

Gardner, H. (1991). *The unschooled mind: How children think and how
schools should teach.* New York, NY: Basic Books.

Gardner, H. (1993). *Multiple intelligences: The theory in practice.* New
York, NY: Basic Books.

Silver, H. F., Strong, R. W., & Perini, M. J. (2000). *So each may learn: Integrating learning styles and multiple intelligences.* Alexandria, VA: Association for Supervision and Curriculum Development.

2

Bridging the Gap: Improving Graduation Rates in a Degree Completion Program

Sean Warner

Although degree completion programs may best describe how many colleges and universities organize their adult learner programs, there may be an inherent weakness in the design of some of these programs, especially if they utilize a cohort model. Degree completion programs imply that entering students have already taken some college credit, and that the programs' purpose is to help students finish what they started. However, in some instances, they only offer coursework to cover the last 35–50 semester credits of a degree. They assume that students will transfer in having already had the first two years of college, if not more. Many degree completion programs have a minimum number of transfer hours that a student must complete prior to admission. Furthermore, students are often expected to complete coursework in key areas, particularly in general education. As a result, such programs are sometimes geared only toward meeting the requirements for a major (e.g., business administration, computer information systems, nursing, etc.).

Since these programs are often lock-stepped, with students forming cohort groups that are sustained the entire length of the program, this design can create a paradox since, for many of the students, a degree completion program does not automatically lead to the completion of the student's degree. For example, a degree may comprise 120–128 semester credits. If a student transfers 60 credits into a degree completion program, that leaves 40 required credit hours still to complete to satisfy the degree requirements of the cohort, meaning the student will require an additional 20–25 credits in order to graduate. But the structure of some programs may prevent a student from accomplishing this objective. The emphasis of these programs is often so heavily on the *program* completion that the idea of *graduation* completion may sometimes get lost.

Most programs recognize this problem and solve it by offering a variety of ways to help the students bridge their hours. Prior learning credit is one alternative. Schools accept credit from the military, corporate, or other organizational training programs. Another solution is some type of prior learning assessment, where a student can obtain credit for learning gained through informal life experiences, hobbies, life transitions, or other events. Standardized tests such as the CLEP (College-Level Examination Program) are also typically available. Some schools allow adult learners to "test out" so that students may document their knowledge for individual courses.

In order to bridge the credit gap, adult learners may take coursework from other universities or community colleges while they are enrolled in their degree completion program. For many students, there are convenience- and price-related advantages associated with these options, though some schools enforce caps on the number of hours—and when they are taken, from other schools.

The Problem

Despite the multiple options available to adult learners, many do not take advantage of them. While adult learners will try to maximize the number of credits they can transfer in from their corporate and training experiences, many will ignore programs such as CLEP. Often, no matter how hard faculty and advisors promote a portfolio assessment program, students will choose to limit how many prior learning essays they write. Similarly, some adult learners avoid taking any online courses.

Because it is difficult to know exactly what causes the reluctance to seek the best options when obtaining degree completion, it is difficult to know how to deal with the problem. Yet the issue is very important. Terminology itself may be an issue. If we describe ourselves as offering a degree *completion* program, we have an obligation to help students complete their degrees, though this is sometimes ignored. And those of us in

accelerated degree completion programs presumably also have an obligation to help our adult learners complete their programs as quickly as
possible. If a program gains a reputation for not responding to student
needs in lieu of programmatic consideration, their credibility is likely to
be seriously damaged.

Encounters in this regard can be startling and difficult. For instance,
on the second day of my current job at Friends University in Wichita, I received a phone call from a lawyer representing a former student. The
lawyer wanted to know what made his client's program "accelerated." I
quickly came to understand that the terminology that we use can be very
significant indeed.

Although Friends University had most of the mechanisms in place to
enable students to bridge the gap (e.g., prior learning assessment, CLEP,
credit by examination), I became concerned when I learned that a number
of our students were not graduating in a timely fashion, even though they
had completed the program segments successfully. In response, we decided to systematically address the issue and improve the graduation rates
of those students who had completed their cognate requirements but who
had yet to graduate.

Some Solutions

To gain perspective, we initially spent a great deal of time talking informally to three sets of constituents involved with our program: existing students, students who had completed their programs but who had not yet
graduated, and students who had completed their programs and who had
also graduated. Then we developed a two-part strategy. We committed to
providing students different and more learning options to help them graduate, and we determined that we could reduce cost and inconvenience—
the two obstacles most cited by adult learners.

We formally tested the two concepts and found that they reflected the
feelings of *all* the students involved, not just those who had not graduated.
We found that even those adult learners who had successfully graduated
reported that they had encountered some confusion about issues they had
to resolve in order to graduate.

It was those students who had not graduated who most concerned us.
We told them up front, when they were applying for admission, that they
would need to gain additional credits before they could graduate. We told

them about these additional credits when they had been accepted into the program. We repeated the information during their first courses, when they were actually involved in a degree-planning process. In fact, they were specifically asked to identify the manner in which they would gain the additional credit, but they didn't fully comprehend, until fairly late in their program, that they needed to assume responsibility for these courses. They apparently rationalized that it was too late for them to do what was necessary to complete the program, so they procrastinated. Many students could barely pay for the courses within the program and additional tuition was impossible. We realized that we had to make some fundamental changes in order to address these issues.

We tried to deal with the problem on a number of levels, recognizing that if we were to be successful, it would require a comprehensive and systemic approach to the problem.

The first change was aimed at the message we would give to the candidates before enrolling in our programs. We could have simply changed the admission requirement, and not allowed students to enroll until they had completed all of their courses other than those offered as "degree completion." However, our intention was to increase service to our students.

Consequently, we chose to work with the admissions office to create an explicit message for potential adult learners in our program. We selected a new brochure which listed all of the options available to students who needed to complete coursework outside of their specific degree program. We indicated the appropriate contact person and explicit steps involved. As a result, incoming adult learners would be made aware of what they had to do in order to graduate.

The vice president for admissions also quickly recognized that her area needed to initiate other basic changes. New forms were created that her division and the registrar's office used to inform students of the degree requirements they met, and those they still required. They spent much time redesigning admission forms and literature to reflect the new emphasis.

This was no easy task, and required a great deal of cooperation from the admissions office. Indeed, what we really required was a change of culture. The admissions staff would no longer be able to just emphasize how easy and convenient our programs were. Their message needed to extend beyond the simple concept of the convenience of attending class for once a week for 20 months. Ultimately, our success was due to their being willing to own the problem themselves, and understand that they had to be part of the solution. It would have been impossible for us to simply mandate this change. It could only have been implemented from within admissions, and supported at the highest levels of their leadership.

Our second change was to remove some of the obstacles that prevented our students from taking full advantage of the services we had in place to bridge the graduation gap. We decided, for example, to discontinue our practice of charging students a per-credit fee for the prior-learning essays that they submitted. Our research indicated that this fee was a major reason that so few of our students took advantage of the option, and why, even if they did, they didn't maximize the opportunity.

Our solution was to remove this per-credit fee and instead charge all students a flat service fee for assessment, allowing them to take up to the maximum 30 credits granted for prior learning "for free." A student focus group suggested this approach, as we chose to address student perceptions. Of course, this type of decision required approval and support from the vice president for administration and finance, and would not have been successful without it. Institutional support at the highest levels was essential.

The third change was in the way we used our academic advisors. We had not been using them proactively, so we repositioned them to become more critical players in our effort. Their role had been reactive and logistical, dealing with individual student concerns such as adding or dropping specific classes, reentering a cohort group, dropping a cohort group, or dealing with class absences. Our decision in this regard was based on research that demonstrated the value of good advising in successful adult learning programs (Wlodkowski, Mauldin, & Campbell, 2002).

To get the most from our effort, we took advantage of the cohort system already in place. The cohort system gives an institution some advantages. It allows each cohort member's progress, or lack of progress, to be closely monitored. This way, an advisor should always know a student's program status and how many classes remain to be completed.

Our program directors had often noted an informal rule of thumb for each cohort where it split into three groups. The first third would be made up of those students who were self-directed, and who had already met all the degree requirements they needed outside their program. The second group would comprise those students who had not completed their degree requirements outside of their program, but who knew what they had to do, and were in the process of following through. The third group would contain students who had a number of degree requirements to meet outside their programs, but who had little idea of how to achieve closure.

In our new design, we deliberately assigned one advisor to each cohort. This meant that an advisor's load was no longer an amorphous mass of students, but was instead tied to a number of cohorts to manage. In this model, each advisor was expected to advise a cohort during its existence. Each advisor could therefore get to know—indeed, was required to know—the cohort's characteristics, and particularly which students needed the most help. The advisors were asked at the time of a cohort's formation to prepare a chart that showed the degree requirements that remained for each member of the group.

Given an average cohort size of no more than 20 students, the advisor could instantly identify the progress for each student. We decided to set up an "advisor visit schedule," where an advisor would be required to visit a cohort a certain number of times during its existence so we could provide continuity, ongoing service, and attention. We could emphasize, in a different and more powerful way than before, the program completion/graduation completion dilemma to our students. In fact, we coupled this effort with regularly scheduled visits from the program director and dean, so that we were more accessible but could also reinforce our support for the students to complete all their studies.

We estimated that each cohort needed to be formally met by an advisor no more than five or six times during its 18-month existence. We reasoned that each visit would primarily concentrate on only five or six students, all of whom would be known to the advisor and who would have been working with them between visits.

A final change was introduced in the form of a new Bridge Program. Previously, we had something in place but it was ineffective. It was inconvenient, it cost too much, and it didn't offer the students the subjects they wanted to take. It was supported because it allowed the institution to believe that it was addressing the problem of graduation rates, and that it was the students, rather than the institution, who were to blame if the graduation rates were not high enough.

To be successful, the new Bridge Program would have to be affordable, offer coursework that would interest students, and be offered in a format that the students would find convenient. Our solution was to create a series of Saturday workshops which would be offered to the students "at cost." The response of the senior administration was very positive.

They immediately approved the low tuition rate. This reflected their essential belief that improving the graduation rates was an institutional priority, and that as long as the university did not lose money on any new program, the college could charge whatever was appropriate. This helped reinforce the importance of the issue to all members of the university community. Consequently, we encountered a renewed spurt of interest in the project from faculty and others. Though a bit of a gamble, this strategy turned out to be justified. The new program never lost money, even at its inception, when some of the original workshop content ideas were not widely accepted by the students.

We discovered that while the issue of content was important, there were other factors as well. Over the first four months of the Bridge Program, more than two-thirds of the workshops were cancelled for lack of enrollment, in spite of the fact that the topics chosen were all suggested by the students. In addition, none of the online courses proposed gained enough enrollment to be offered—all were cancelled. Students had asked for three-credit workshops to be held on four or five successive Saturdays, but these too did not make the minimum enrollment required, and all of them were cancelled. What survived after the first six months was one concept: a one-credit workshop, offered on a Saturday from 8:30 a.m.–5:00 p.m. It was this concept that we ultimately adopted.

The workshops received some excellent public relations. A special flyer was created with a distinctive logo and layout. Mailings were sent to all enrolled students, as well as to those students who had completed their degree program but who had not yet graduated. The dean and others made classroom visits to all the enrolled cohorts, informed them of the idea, and asked the students to take advantage of the new program.

Lessons Learned

The lessons we learned are relevant when launching a new program, as in the Bridge Program, or when trying to solve the broader issue of graduation rates in general.

- Use the mission of the organization to define your operation. It helps, of course, to have a formal mission statement, but even if this does not exist, concentrate on your identity and mission. This is particularly important in degree *completion* programs. If that is how we advertise ourselves and how we describe ourselves, then we really do need to focus on that word, and have a sense of obligation to our students. Our institutional "blunder" was not recognizing what we were really about, and therefore not creating the appropriate systems in response.

- When trying to solve a problem such as increasing graduation rates, one has to think it through systematically and on a number of levels. For instance, we identified three layers of change that had to be addressed. The problem had to be addressed at the macro level first, and then further broken down into smaller and smaller parts. We would not have been successful if, for example, we had only put the new Bridge Program into place, or just decided to create another admissions brochure, or change the way the advisors interacted with the students.

- Understand the strengths and weaknesses of the people on whom you rely in your organization, so you can draw on their support. This will require flexibility and insight, but any project will only succeed if you can call on the support and assistance of others.

- Be prepared to tread on toes, and be strong when necessary. In the case described above, we initially encountered a great deal of opposition. Our success required a willingness to overlook criticism and to persevere.

- Retain as much flexibility as possible, and be prepared for the unanticipated.

- When innovating, if something doesn't work initially, keep trying. It took nearly six months of trying to determine market needs before we decided to only implement the one-day workshop idea, ignore online instruction, and concentrate on the subject themes that we did. (A year later, however, it is interesting to note that students are asking for the same workshop subjects as they originally did, and that, for whatever reason, they are now actually enrolling in them.)

- Look for opportunities everywhere. When building new programs, be positive, optimistic, and opportunistic in all things.

- Change is always stressful. In our case, profound change appeared to generate profound stress. The impact among stakeholders and individuals intimately involved with our transformation has been particularly damaging in terms of major health issues. Changes in an organization's structure, and particularly in its culture, can therefore be very stressful indeed. The changes introduced to improve our graduation rates occurred while the institution was undertaking a broader reorganization of its entire academic division. This alone increased the stress level of all involved, but the combination was fairly devastating.

Conclusion

None of the individual steps we took to bridge the gap are necessarily best practices. On their own, none of them will lead to an automatic improvement in an institution's graduation rates. Creating a new Bridge Program of Saturday workshops will not necessarily do the job on its own either, any more than altering the wording of admissions brochures, or changing the fees for selected student activities.

However, we believe that taken together, all of the steps outlined above are illustrative of best practice activity. The best practice here lies in the fact that the institution collectively decided that bridging the gap was an important issue that had to be addressed, and further, that it could *only* be addressed collectively, with the involvement of the whole university community and not just the individual college. Had the institution decided that the matter was one for the college alone to deal with, it is doubtful that we would have been able to make the necessary change of culture nor achieve the results that we did.

Changes like these have to be constantly improved upon and further developed. The Bridge workshop program, for example, is still a work in progress. But the foundation we were able to establish has served us well, and I hope you may draw some insights from our experiences.

Reference

Wlodkowski, R. J., Mauldin, J. E., & Campbell, S. (2002). *Early exit: Understanding adult attrition in accelerated and traditional postsecondary programs.* Indianapolis, IN: Lumina Foundation.

3

Program Planning and Review in Adult Higher Education: Using Program Models Effectively

Patricia R. Brewer

Program planning in adult higher education is as critical today as it was in the 1960s and 1970s, when many colleges and universities began to experiment with alternative programming structures for nontraditional students. With the variety of program options now available to learners, and with the growing number of adult degree programs marketed through consultants and contractors, how can program planners administer exemplary *best practice models* to work successfully within the unique colleges and universities in which they are housed?

It's been many years since I've done program planning from the ground up, and much of the program planning literature wasn't even written when I began working with adult programs in the late 1970s. And yet, as a practitioner who has worked in a number of adult higher education programs, I'm drawn to the good-sense approach and operational balance that programming planning literature provides. I am convinced that structure can improve the quality of the programs that we offer to adult students, and I think that working with program models can uncover and protect the rich culture of adult learning on which good institutions rely when educating adult learners. The practical truth is this: Significant outreach to adult learners in higher education only occurs within well-designed programmatic structures. The importance of coherent program planning and delivery cannot be underestimated.

Program Planning Literature

In 1956, Peter Siegle and James Whipple prepared a report for the annual meeting of the Association of University Evening Colleges. *New Directions in Programming for University Adult Education* provided descriptions of new and innovative efforts to serve the growing population of adults who were returning to university study. The authors suggested that the models of significant kinds of ideas might be transferable to other institutions and could provide information on which future programs might be based. Included in the paper were programs in the liberal arts, professional continuing education for managers, and even a laboratory college for adults. The purpose of Siegle and Whipple's paper was not to be prescriptive about how programs should be planned. Rather, they described energy and innovation in the developing field and encouraged growth and challenge for the kinds of programs that would serve this particular group of learners.

A review of program planning literature today reveals precise descriptions of the various steps that are suggested for program planning. There are often ties to adult learning theory and indicators of how a particular model complements or enhances that theory. And as the profession's understanding of program planning has developed, there are recent writings on theoretical aspects of program planning and how understanding that theory contributes to program success.

An abundance of literature exists on the topic of program planning, but two recent pieces provide especially good resources for practitioners. *Developing Programs in Adult Education*, a 2002 second edition by Boone, Safrit, and Jones provides a comprehensive review of program planning literature, beginning with Ralph Tyler's (1949) *Basic Principles of Curriculum and Instruction* and ending with Thomas Sork's (2000) chapter in the *Handbook of Adult and Continuing Education*. For each model included in the text there is a description of three key components including planning, design and implementation, and evaluation and implementation. A summary chart provides a compare-and-contrast thumbnail sketch of each model and summarizes key components provided in the narrative descriptions. The text then turns to the authors' conceptual programming model—a model in which the technical components are enhanced with philosophical considerations and assumptions about adult learners that are often implicit in program planning. By providing sound information for new planners and best practice challenges for those who would use it to rethink or review an existing program, the text is a comprehensive tool for program planners. For an all-inclusive overview of program development in adult education, it would be difficult to find a more exhaustive resource in a single volume.

In "Planning Educational Programs" (Sork, 2000), the author traces what he describes as a brief genealogy of planning theory. In addition to technical descriptions of program planning models, Sork includes linkages to particular philosophies of adult learning, notably Malcolm Knowles's (1950, 1970) principles of adult learning with its distinctively humanist flavor and Wilson's and Cervero's (1996) approach to negotiating issues of power and control inherent in all program planning.

From the 1950 *Informal Adult Education* through various iterations of the theory of andragogy, Sork notes the influential nature of Knowles's writings on program planning literature. It is generally understood that Knowles's writings include a series of descriptors about adult learners and a set of guidelines for practice. Central components of Knowles's theory are self-directedness, a focus on experiential learning, learner reliance on past experiences, adult motivation to learn, and a goal orientation associated with problem solving. These elements constitute the framework that most adults bring to the learning activity. In adult higher education, Knowles's principles are evident in a number of program initiatives: learning contracts, self-designed degrees, and prior learning assessment programs.

Sork also discusses the work of Wilson and Cervero (1996) who have urged a better comprehension of the political context in the "people work" that is inherent in program planning. Calling for an understanding that "real people plan programs in complex organizations, which have traditions, political relationships, and needs and interests that profoundly influence the planning process" (p. 6), Wilson and Cervero criticize the existing literature for its reliance upon technical aspects of program planning. They note that experienced planners learn different lessons about planning programs in particular contexts and rely upon past learning experiences to negotiate political issues inherent in program structure and delivery. According to the authors, the culture of the organization itself and the power relationships evidenced within it often limit good practice in program planning.

Sork then introduces his own model for program planning, one that includes the following basic elements: analyze the context and the learner community, justify and focus planning, clarify intentions, prepare the instructional plan, prepare the administrative plan, develop a summative evaluation plan. Unlike most planning models that are displayed in a linear sequence, Sork settles on a questions-based approach to planning that lends itself to a reiterative use, either for initial program planning or for analysis of an existing program. In Sork's model, three domains frame the questions that are asked about program planning. The author notes the need for technical capabilities in program planning—for example, conducting needs assessment, allocation of resources, program review, and other skills. Like Wilson and Cervero, Sork recommends attention to the sociopolitical domain of the organization in which the program is housed. In introducing the third, ethical domain, Sork challenges planners to a basic level of ethical responsibility by noting that all technical decisions, from participant list to program evaluation, have moral implications for practice.

In adult higher education, responding to questions in the political and ethical domains may prove to be a special challenge. In the 50 years that have passed since Siegle and Whipple provided early descriptions of adult programs, adult learners have become the new majority in most colleges and universities, far outnumbering their traditional counterparts. Yet, as noted in "The Politics of Neglect: Adult Learners in Higher Education" (Sissel, Hansman, & Kasworm, 2001), adult learners are not a celebrated constituency group and continue to be relegated to lower status in the higher education caste system.

Uncovering Program Theory

Since the mid-1990s, my professional work has focused on adult undergraduate programs and how practitioners in those programs conceptualize and carry out their work. Uncovering what Patton (1990) calls "program theory of action" has provided an opportunity for me to better understand how programs operate and why a program develops in a particular way. Influenced by the writings of Usher (1989) and Usher and Bryant (1989), I have found value in deconstructing the operational aspects of a program in order to find links between theories of adult learning and how those theories are evident in practice.

My own study, conducted in 1998, of Towne University (pseudonym) uncovered a distinctive program theory of action that revealed many of

Caffarella's (1994) internal contextual factors related to program structure, people, and culture. Embedded in the program theory was an ideology that provided philosophical underpinnings consistent with the mission of the university and goals for learners that could be aligned with adult learning theory. Teaching methods reflected adult learning principles and acknowledged adult learner characteristics. There were, within the unit, dedicated services and learner supports particularly useful for adult populations, including flexible course delivery and a supportive faculty. More importantly, these elements of program theory resulted in a strong culture of adult learning that was promised to students and implemented by individual faculty members. Significant to the program's success within a traditional university structure, the growing program was eventually housed in a dedicated school for adult learners and was headed by a dean.

The organizational structure of dean and school significantly contributed to the culture of adult learning that developed at Towne. The familiar symbol and responsibilities associated with deanship helped to align curricular initiatives with comparable structures throughout the university. Many of the faculty members were not initially familiar with adult learning theory. Eventually, theoretical expertise and skills associated with practitioner research became linked to promotion and tenure initiatives in the adult school, as the dean's position allowed for a link between what Boyle (1981) calls educational ends and maintenance ends of the program.

However, the program theory at Towne University wasn't the result of any particular program planning model. Instead, the program was constructed over a number of years and was influenced by a variety of internal and external factors, including changes in university personnel and market-driven responses to adult higher education. Along the way, the adult program at Towne benefited from the influence of a few key faculty members who were interested in adult learning theory, modeled their practice to serve adult learners, and shared their ideas with others. Program theory was not the result of explicit program planning for adult learners, or even an acknowledgement that program planning for adults might need to be distinctive from how the university planned for traditional undergraduates. Instead, it was implicit, and was revealed only in descriptions of how the majority of faculty and learners within the program conducted the teaching and learning exchange.

Tensions exist in any organizational structure, and the program theory of action identified for the adult school did little to uncover how the broader university came to understand the central functions of program planning and administration. More importantly, the thick program description that focused exclusively on behaviors within the adult school failed to explore the level at which the university would embrace the central principles upon which the program was based. Program theory of action is fluid and changes as internal and external contexts of programs change. In recent years, an integrative plan for serving adult learners has replaced the adult school model; the program theory of action identified in 1998 has given way to a revised version today.

Sork (2000) noted that program planning literature is rightfully critiqued for being too technical and contrived and not particularly relevant to experienced practitioners. Given those limitations, uncovering program theory of action can be an important first step in understanding, and subsequently evaluating, adult programs. Then, faced with "people work" and its inherent conflict and negotiation, practitioners can rely upon a theoretical and practical foundation for making programmatic decisions.

Making Use of Planning Models

If we can't make use of planning models for actually planning programs for adult learners, how can models be used beneficially? For practitioners who inherit rather than create adult degree programs, the tasks of program evaluation and modification surpass those activities associated with program planning. Accrediting agencies and state legislatures are demanding an accounting of program benefits and successes that is different than what has been expected in the past. New deans or program directors are often faced with problems to solve, and significant programmatic change may be seen as the solution. But occasionally, major modifications that appear to provide good solutions to operational or organizational problems run the risk of diminishing the very foundation that makes a program strong. Uncovering program theory is one way to guide programmatic decisions; using program planning models for program evaluation is another.

During the 2003–2004 academic year, I was engaged in several evaluation efforts. In each case, selecting an appropriate planning model helps to frame the nature of the program and the kind of evaluation most relevant for its context.

The first evaluation project looked at how well our assessment steering committee had framed the year's activities for meeting guidelines from the Higher Learning Commission of the North Central Association of Colleges and Schools (HLC/NCA). This end-of-year evaluation relied heavily upon the committee's ability to be proficient in organizing assessment goals, providing faculty development opportunities, and moving along the assessment agenda at our institution. The program planning model developed by Boyle (1981) had been adapted to the context of this committee's work and allowed the committee to focus on the technical implementation of the program and how to improve upon those instrumental steps.

The second project was a self-study of the university's prior learning assessment program. Sork's (2000) question-based approach to planning was used for this initiative. Sork's model is particularly useful because of the three domains that must be explored in such a program. Aside from the technical aspects of best practice in prior learning assessment that have been identified (Middle States Commission on Higher Education, 1996), the underlying assumptions about prior learning assessment are laden with issues of power and control, as noted in "Prior Learning Assessment: The Quiet Revolution" (Thomas, 2000). Making the implicit explicit in terms of the sociopolitical domain may help to ensure responsible program revision in light of the often conflicted understandings of experiential learning and how to evaluate and honor it. "Honor" in this case is a value-laden term, so Sork's emphasis on ethics and moral discourse will further solidify a comprehensive program review.

A third set of evaluative activities allowed me to visit adult degree programs in three different states as part of college and university reaccreditation efforts. In these instances, professional organizations provided excellent resources for program planning and evaluation. HLC/NCA (2000) has identified practice guidelines for adult degree completion programs and has recommended *Serving Adult Learners in Higher Education: Principles of Effectiveness* (Council for Adult and Experiential Learning [CAEL], 2000) and *Principles of Good Practice for Alternative and External Degree Programs for Adults* (American Council on Education & The Alliance: An Association for Alternative Degree Programs for Adults, 1990) as a framework for institutional self study. The Adult Learning Focused Institution (ALFI) study, undertaken by CAEL with the support of the Lumina Foundation and technical assistance from the National Center for Higher Education Management Systems and Noel-Levitz, further challenges colleges and universities to critically review instructional and support services that will benefit adult learners in higher education programs.

Program Planning and Lessons Learned

I can think of nothing more critical to the success of adult learners in the academy than the foundation and structure of the programs that serve them. Aside from the technical aspects of program planning, the underlying assumptions of what it means to learn in adulthood, within the structure of the university, is the most significant question that can be answered if we are to serve our adult learners in best practice settings. Since competition abounds for maintaining successful degree programs in adult higher education, what lessons can be gleaned from trying to understand the role of the adult learner in your own college or university setting?

First, best practice programs are always found within organizations that have a stated mission and philosophy of serving adult learners. Given today's marketplace, "serving adult learners" is a tempting activity, one that is often a creative and gratifying experience for the practitioner. Most adult higher education programs that have developed over the past twenty-five years, however, do not emanate from a college mission that may be a century old or more. The lucrative nature of adult programs makes them fiscally attractive, and so mission is often rewritten to include service to adults. For institutions that continue to have a more traditional mindset and are not open to reinterpreting the nature of teaching, learning, and student services, adult programs become little more than cash cows for supporting the traditional programs. As a result of such practices, the integrity of the program and the university is often called into question. Technical skills in program planning and evaluation won't create a well-defined philosophy of adult education or ensure a culture of adult learning, both of which are critical to ongoing success of a program. And given the reality of program change that is often influenced by sociopolitical circumstances within the university, successful negotiation of power and conflict must be guided by an authentic understanding of what it means to provide meaningful educational experiences to adult students.

Second, it is important for practitioners to have a solid foundation in the theories associated with adult learning, development, and program planning. In adult higher education, learning is a collaborative effort between the learner and the instructor. Both are better served by understanding the theoretical underpinnings of the teaching-learning experience. In fact, I would argue that some of the theories associated with adult learning (for example, reflection on experience) become invalid if they are not part of the educational environment that both learner and teacher embrace.

Third, for the reflective practitioner, understanding program theory of action is a precursor to program evaluation. Program theory of action, the combination of what we say versus what we do in adult programs, requires data collection from many program players (learners, faculty, administrators) in order to provide a sufficient description of how the program works. Understanding how a program functions within the larger institutional context is an important first step in quality improvement.

Program planning models can be used selectively for program evaluation. Program models have developed in varied contexts and can be used judiciously for different purposes. Even in adult higher education, there are distinctions to be made between degree-completion programs and professional continuing education initiatives. Faculty development programs and committee work are both examples of adult learning experiences; after all, faculty who are part of adult degree programs are themselves adult learners. Being able to evaluate the effectiveness of programs in these various contexts requires knowledge of program planning models and a willingness to use models appropriately in best practice settings.

Lessons Learned

- Colleges and universities have a dual responsibility to the students that they serve. In addition to maintaining curricular integrity within the disciplines offered by the institution, they must also offer instruction and provide services in ways that are contextually appropriate for the learner. This requirement is as important in adult higher education programs as it is in traditional undergraduate education.

- Programs that are designed to meet the needs of the adult learner have a special responsibility to frame the adult program within an agreed-upon foundation, or a theoretical underpinning, for the teaching-learning experience.

- Adult degree programs often have the need to produce revenue. For many adult degree programs, their continued existence depends upon the ability to maintain innovative and cost-effective programs.

- Adult degree programs are not immune to calls for accountability and demonstration of quality through assessment of learning. Program planning models can be used effectively for program review and revision, ensuring that colleges and universities create local best practice examples for serving adult learners.

References

American Council on Education & The Alliance: An Association for Alternative Degree Programs for Adults. (1990). *Principles of good practice for alternative and external degree programs for adults.* Washington, DC: American Council on Education. Retrieved September 15, 2004, from http://www.ahea.org/ pogp.htm

Boone, E. J., Safrit, R. D., & Jones, J. (2002). *Developing programs in adult education: A conceptual programming model* (2nd ed.). Prospect Heights, IL: Waveland Press.

Boyle, P. (1981). *Planning better programs.* New York, NY: McGraw-Hill.

Brewer, P. R. (1998). *Program theory of action and adult learning: A case study from adult higher education.* Ann Arbor, MI: UMI Dissertation Services.

Caffarella, R. (1994). *Planning programs for adult learners.* San Francisco, CA: Jossey-Bass.

Council for Adult and Experiential Learning. (2000). *Serving adult learners in higher education: Principles of effectiveness* (Executive summary). Chicago, IL: Author. Retrieved September 15, 2004, from http://www.cael.org/alfi/PDF%20files/Summary%20of%20Alfi%20 Principles%20of%20Effectiveness.pdf

Higher Learning Commission of the North Central Association of Colleges and Schools. (2000). *Principles of good practice in adult degree completion programs.* Chicago, IL: Author.

Knowles, M. S. (1950). *Informal adult education: A guide for administrators, leaders, and teachers.* New York, NY: Association Press.

Knowles, M. S. (1970). *The modern practice of adult education.* Chicago, IL: Follett.

Middle States Commission on Higher Education. (1996). *Assessing prior learning for credit.* Philadelphia, PA: Author.

Patton, M. Q. (1990). *Qualitative evaluation and research methods.* London, England: Sage.

Siegle, P., & Whipple, J. (1956). *New directions in programming for university adult education.* New York, NY: Center for the Study of Liberal Education for Adults.

Sissel, P. A., Hansman, C. A., & Kasworm, C. E. (2001). The politics of neglect: Adult learners in higher education. In C. A. Hansman & P. A. Sissel (Eds.), *New directions for adult and continuing education: No. 91. Understanding and negotiating the political landscape of adult education* (pp. 17–27). San Francisco, CA: Jossey-Bass.

Sork, T. J. (2000). Planning educational programs. In A. L. Wilson & E. R. Hayes (Eds.), *Handbook of adult and continuing education* (New ed., pp. 171–190). San Francisco, CA: Jossey-Bass and the American Association for Adult and Continuing Education.

Thomas, A. M. (2000). Prior learning assessment: The quiet revolution. In A. L. Wilson & E. R. Hayes (Eds.), *Handbook of adult and continuing education* (pp. 508–522). San Francisco, CA: Jossey-Bass and the American Association for Adult and Continuing Education.

Tyler, R. W. (1949). *Basic principles of curriculum and instruction.* Chicago, IL: University of Chicago Press.

Usher, R. (1989). Locating adult education in the practical. In B. Bright (Ed.), *Theory and practice in the study of adult education: The epistemological debate* (pp. 65–93). London, England: Routledge.

Usher, R., & Bryant, I. (1989). *Adult education as theory, practice and research: The captive triangle.* London, England: Routledge.

Wilson, A. L., & Cervero, R. M. (1996). Paying attention to the people work when planning educational programs for adults. In R. M. Cervero & A. L. Wilson (Eds.), *New directions for adult and continuing education: No. 69. What really matters in adult education: Lessons in negotiating power and interests* (pp. 5–14). San Francisco, CA: Jossey-Bass.

Part II

Defining Moments in Adult Learner Programs

4

Strategic Partnerships: Successfully Managing Collaborative Ventures in Adult Education

Bruce Pietrykowski

Serving the educational needs of adult learners of the 21st century means staying attentive to economic and political changes in an increasingly global society. As the world continues to become more complex, the sheer diversity of adult learning needs is immense and increasing. Programs in adult literacy historically met the needs of one segment of adults while industrial unions have championed technical training and skill upgrading for workers laid off due to technical change and global competition. Yet, forces that traditionally affected blue-collar workers are now also confronting white-collar workers in financial services, computer programming, and software development. Among this white-collar population, programs in job training and retraining are now joined by efforts to encourage continuous learning. In response to this growth in the demand for lifelong learning, many universities have discovered that strategic partnerships provide the best way to provide educational programs for an increasingly diverse adult learner population (Johnson & Cooper, 1999; Martin & Samuels, 2002; Meister, 2001).

In this chapter, I will offer advice on how to identify, develop, support, and nurture strategic partnerships for adult learner programs. I draw upon my experience as associate dean and director of an adult distance learning partnership involving a major union and a multinational corporation. At each step I offer a set of best practices for accomplishing goals relevant to these activities.

Knowing Your Institution Is Key to Successful Strategic Partnerships

Knowing your institution goes beyond simply knowing your mission. Articulating a mission is important, but mission statements are place- and time-bound, so campus retreats and revisioning sessions are useful to reevaluate the mission and revise objectives. Being willing to adapt to changing circumstances is always important.

Examining the Life Cycle of Your Institution

Strategic partnerships inevitably alter relationships within the university by changing expectations, increasing uncertainty, or generally revising the rules of the game. Different types of partnerships are more or less threatening to entrenched interests, but all partnerships require flexibility and accommodation on the part of individuals and groups. In order to ascertain the ability of your institution to successfully implement a strategic partnership, it is important to know your institution's stage in its life cycle and its place in the political economic environment.

Recognizing the life cycle of a college or university means understanding that an institution is a complex network of relationships between students, staff, faculty, and administrators. Each of these groups has its own dominant cohort that represents a certain stage of the life cycle. For example, demographic shifts can lead to a subtle or dramatic transformation of the student body over time (Miller, 1999). Knowing the ways in which student attitudes and needs shift—and being able to document such information—is crucial to understanding the relevance of the stated mission as well as the areas where strategic partnerships can assist your current and future students.

Identifying the Dominant Group in Your Institution

Paying attention to shifting demographics in the ranks of faculty and staff can alert you to potential needs as well as opportunities for partnering. I will use as an example the opportunity my university had to partner in an adult distance learning program. Senior members in several relevant departments dominated the faculty in the college. Senior faculty were a large and politically powerful cohort that took pride in the history and mission of the college. It seemed unlikely that the cohort would support new instructional technology. Instead (so I thought), early adopters of the new distance learning instructional technologies were more likely to be found among the ranks of junior faculty. In general terms this might have been the case. But we were able to enlist the support of a few influential senior faculty members and ultimately, they made the difference. The key to the successful recruitment of this core of senior faculty lay in part with the target audience—adult students who were also union members. These older faculty members were willing to climb the steep learning curve associated with new technology because they saw a personal and a political benefit. They empathized with working-class students who were otherwise unable to get a college degree. Indeed, since the average age of students in the program was a generation older than the typical college student, there developed a sense of solidarity between the faculty and students over the challenge of coming to terms with the brave new world of distance education. Had I scanned the institution's life cycle and focused on senior faculty at the outset, the process of institutionalizing distance learning on our campus may well have been easier.

Knowing the Stage of Your Institution's Product Life Cycle

A university is a complex institution reflecting many constituent parts. Viewed in this way, the university can be seen as a producer of educational goods and services. The education that universities produce has its own life cycle. Economists use the term "product life cycle" to illustrate the dependence of a product or service on the size and rate of expansion of its market. For example, in the first half of the 20th century, colleges were limited in size and scale. Not surprisingly, the market for college education was also limited in size. As college became more desirable and more affordable, the market for higher education grew. The initial motives for expansion emerged because of increases in income, decreases in price, demographic growth (baby booms reflecting census spurts), and through the implementation of subsidies by the public and private sectors (e.g., scholarships, financial aid, and corporate tuition reimbursement programs).

Over time, however, in the absence of a baby boom, the allure and affordability of higher education reaches a point of saturation. One solution to the problem of saturation is to adopt product innovations in the hope of again expanding the market for education. The use of new distance learning technologies is one example of product innovation.

Employing technology to expand the reach of adult education programs is one way to stem the downside of the product life cycle—market saturation and product maturity. Similarly, partnerships can be a means of expanding the range of your market by providing educational services to adults who may not otherwise go to college.

Using the product life cycle to assess project and program placement is fairly simple. We can survey our degree programs and identify each program's stage in its life cycle. For instance, we might find that a new degree program in applied economics is just starting to expand and is clearly in the growth stage of its life cycle, whereas the creative writing program is in the mature stage of its life cycle. But we are not alone in our projections. Our counterparts at neighboring colleges are undertaking the same type of analysis. Therefore, we need to think about strategic partnerships within the context of a dynamic, interactive, and competitive adult education environment.

Developing Strategic Partnerships in a Competitive Environment

The use of partnerships requires cooperation and trust. Yet these cooperative, trust-based relationships often increase competition between non-partner schools. In eras of lean budgets and aggressive enrollment planning goals, there is enormous pressure to see others merely as competitors in a zero-sum game—the student they get is the student we lose. Nevertheless, in a dynamic environment, it's vital to remember that today's competitors may be tomorrow's partners. Keeping the shared values of higher education in mind can temper the impulse to leap into potentially unproductive forms of competition. Distance learning partnerships in higher education provide good examples.

Throughout the 1990s distance learning was the hot new thing in higher education (Paulson, 2002; U.S. Department of Education, 2003). The fact that college courses could be offered to working adults who were unable to attend college due to time and space constraints held great appeal. Add the fact that these additional enrollments did not require any capital expenditures for classroom buildings and you have the makings for a programmatic stampede. As the director of a brand new distance learning program, I had an inside view of these developments.

Creating Strategic Partnerships: A Firsthand Perspective
In 1996, my university entered into a contractual agreement with the union representing a major manufacturing company. The agreement provided a university-style undergraduate degree program for the company's hourly workforce. The following primary institutions (illustrated in Figure 4.1) were included in the agreement: the flagship campus of a major

FIGURE 4.1

Organizational Structure of the Partnerships in an Adult Distance Learning Program

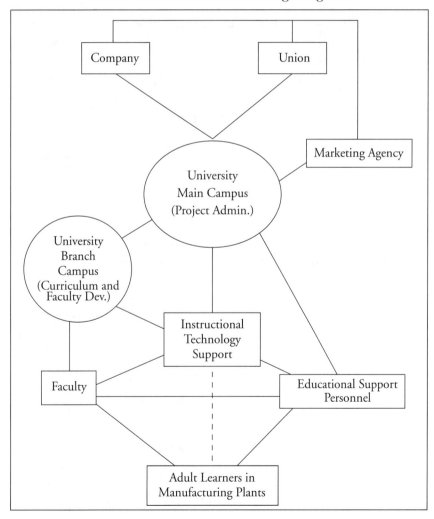

research university, a regional campus in the same university system, the union, and the company. Within the university the participants included an executive director from the flagship campus, a faculty development and curriculum director from the branch campus (the author), administrative and academic support staff from the flagship campus, faculty from the branch campus, and instructional technology staff from the flagship campus. Additional participants included in-plant educational support staff hired from local schools and community colleges, a local educational software development company, and a marketing company to promote the program to workers in selected plants throughout the country.

This large partnership was, in reality, a complex set of customized collaborations. The contract defined the general contours of the primary relationship between the union/company and the university. There was no explicit contract governing the relationship between the flagship campus personnel and those of us at the branch campus. While on paper we all worked in the same university system, in fact, we had never worked together and the two campuses had rarely, if ever, worked this closely on such a large-scale educational endeavor.

The resulting five-year relationship taught me some valuable lessons that I would like to share.

Lessons Learned

Stay Focused on What Is Expected From the Partnership

Strategic partnerships involve more than the subtle and not-so-subtle negotiation over the exchange of resources. Courses are offered, staff time committed, and faculty recruited. In return the nonprofit agency, company, or union helps to recruit qualified students. The exact nature of this exchange can never be completely spelled out in the contract. What happens if the expectations of faculty regarding the quality of student are not met? Or from the students' side, what if there is a mismatch between the content of the courses and their perceived applicability to the world of work? In an adult education partnership, the possibility for dissatisfaction is not limited to the classroom. The adult learner may feel that the company should reward his or her participation in a company-sponsored academic program. On the other hand, the company (union or nonprofit agency) may decide that the education received provides general skills that can be transferred to other jobs if the worker quits or becomes laid off.

Confusion typically stems from lack of clarity or focus on the program's goals. Each participant carries an agenda, but it is important to be clear about that agenda and to be able to acknowledge competing agendas without losing sight of your own objectives.

Don't Let the Partnership Drive the University

The partnership process can be an exhilarating experience. Strategic partnerships are, by their very nature, dynamic and oftentimes innovative ventures. They hold special appeal to those who feel constrained by rule-bound organizational structures. There is a recent trend within some institutions of higher education to encourage and reward entrepreneurial behavior. However, there are real dangers in creating spaces in your organization for unregulated entrepreneurship. Getting caught up in the excitement of charting new territory runs the risk of unintentionally replacing the goals of the institution with the goal of maintaining the partnership.

Partnerships are not always intended to be long lived. When the objective is met, partners should seek amicable closure with a shared desire to reactivate a partnership if and when the opportunity arises. Avoid the temptation to build an empire out of a partnership.

Maintain Communication Loops

As partnerships evolve, there is a natural tendency to shift into automatic pilot mode. After all, developing a partnership involves the establishment of a community of diverse individuals who come together to build trust, a set of common understandings, and a common language. Because of the similarities of background, everyone is likely to understand the problems and shares a common stock of knowledge. The process probably seems effortless. There are bound to be difficulties, but a set of shared background assumptions ensures that everyone understands the rules of the game.

On the other hand, when participants come with different experiences and diverse work cultures, even more effort is likely to be expended interpreting and learning about others in your group. Over time, as you come to understand one another better, you may even begin to speak the same language.

In either instance, there is a tendency to believe that communication can now take place of its own accord without much attention to further interpretation or negotiation of meaning. This response is understandable but potentially dangerous. Such an assumption often leads to complacency and should be resisted. Maintaining communication loops requires that you actively listen to the responses you receive so you can evaluate whether your message is getting through.

One example from my own experience serves to illustrate this point. After months of designing an innovative curriculum that sought to bring a liberal arts education to bear on issues involving engineering and management, we were ready to begin marketing the program to workers in the factory. We all agreed that this would be a rigorous program offered to students through interactive video and web-based instructional technology. Our success in forging a curriculum lulled me into believing that we inhabited a shared-discourse community. However, when it came time to market the program as an academic distance learning program for working adults, serious misunderstandings arose. The distance learning program was touted—rightly so—as being more convenient for students than driving to campus to attend class. Asynchronous distance learning was marketed as even more student-friendly than interactive video. However, the combination of convenience and academic rigor did not always get communicated in a way that allowed us to separate the ease of attending classes from the need for self-discipline and motivation. It was not that there was disagreement over the need to send students this dual message but, because we relied on our imagined discourse community to shoulder the weight, we were unable to quickly develop an effective way of getting that message across. This problem could have been averted if we had monitored the communication loop more carefully.

Partnerships Can Complement, Reinforce, and Strengthen Your Mission

For many years the university in which I work has moved steadily down a path familiar to many administrators, a path of growth and expansion facilitated by enrollment planning goals and the addition of new facilities to accommodate new students and programs. Program expansion at the graduate level has been the primary engine of growth. Strategic partnerships have been formed with employers interested in creating new applied areas of education in the health and transportation sectors. These partnerships are beginning to drive the liberal arts curriculum in ways that mirror the development of industry-sensitive degree programs in engineering and management. This has resulted in enrollment growth. But there are some on campus who question whether graduate education in the liberal arts is consistent with the college's commitment to undergraduate education. Although this issue is by no means unique, its solution challenges many schools of higher learning. Is there a way to engage in growth at the graduate level that benefits the undergraduate teaching and learning experience? This is the challenge that my campus is grappling with. There are few easy answers. Understanding how the mission is facilitated by the enrollment plan is critical to forging and sustaining the right partnerships.

Similarly, new partnerships can be used to validate and make legitimate our most basic and taken-for-granted missions. For example, our foray into adult distance education had the effect of reaffirming our mission to provide high-quality educational opportunities to working adults. It also compelled us to reach out to community colleges to establish articulation agreements that would allow a community college student to move nearly seamlessly into our distance learning degree program. This program motivated us to return to our roots. Our campus was founded primarily as a two-year institution providing upper-division courses in engineering and management. More than 40 years later we developed a degree program which consisted primarily of upper-division courses with a liberal arts focus on issues of work and technology. This gave us the opportunity to reclaim our historical roots and to renew our commitment to our founding mission. Partnerships that allow you to reconnect to and reaffirm your mission may have a special worth. When performing a cost-benefit analysis of a strategic partnership, institutional benefits such as this need to be taken into account.

Partnerships Can Act as Catalysts for Reinventing the University
Depending on the climate for change at your college or university, partnerships offer an opportunity to chart new territory and expand the boundaries of organizational change. This is most visible in attempts to form consortia among colleges and universities to develop shared academic programming in areas such as distance learning. Universitas 21, for example, consists of 17 international universities in Asia, North America, Europe, and Australia. Together with the publishing house Thomson Learning, they have banded together to offer courses and degree programs (Arnone, 2002). The goal is collaboration and profitability. The challenge is to create a set of opportunities that meets a demand while not competing with existing programs offered by member schools. Ventures like this appear to move universities closer to the role of corporations that seek the

highest rate of return on their investments. This, of course, is not new. In the early 20th century, business supported the establishment of schools of commerce at major U.S. universities (Leach, 1993). But extensive reliance on such business partnerships may have the effect of reorienting the university. Some in high education see this as a *fait accompli* and are quick to highlight the benefits inherent in the increasing commercialization of higher education (Duderstadt, 1997–1998) while others are critical of this trend (Arnone, 2002; Aronowitz, 2000; Pietrykowski, 2001).

On the other hand, partnerships could help to shift the focus of adult education away from the model of the isolated student-employee in need of discrete skills and training. For example, the goal espoused by Malcolm Knowles (1962), that adult education should promote the education of communities and organizations, points to an alternative model for adult education. In either case, strategic partnerships can help bring about a change in adult education as it exists today.

Determine How Many Partners Are Too Many

The optimum number of partners is a function of the scope of the project and the particular expertise each participant contributes. As a rule, the more partners, the higher the costs of administration, coordination, and communication. From a revenue perspective, the more participants offering educational opportunities, the larger the scale of enrollments needed to ensure an adequate distribution of revenue to all participants. This all sounds simple. In reality, the strategic partner with the most power will try to vary the number of partners to their advantage. In the case of a single employer or industrial sector, the goal might be to increase the amount of competition among educational providers in order to increase the variety and number of degree offerings. This is where the opportunity to construct a pilot project is useful in developing a personal relationship with your partner. This is also where it makes sense to be among the first to create a partnership opportunity or respond to a request for proposals.

The pilot phase is when you learn the most about the proposed project so that your organization can benefit from its participation. A pilot participant can elevate a university into the status of lead institution when it comes time to expand the number of project participants. Participation in the pilot phase can have some pitfalls, however. For example, a corporate partner testing the waters with a pilot educational initiative may not respond favorably to the typical glitches that can accompany the startup of a new academic program or the marketing of an existing program to a new audience. Since a pilot program may be especially volatile, you will want to carefully assess the merits before making a commitment to enter this phase. It is especially important to be clear about the contractual expectations and the means by which success will be measured.

Redefine Adult Learning for All Stakeholders

Adult educators and administrators know that the way educational opportunities are provided can have a profound effect on students, employers, and labor unions. Joint labor-management educational efforts have been shaped by the practice of adult educators, together with the interests of workers and employers, to define what education means (Aronowitz, 2000; Eurich, 1990; Knowles, 1962). In my own experience, this struggle to define the nature and aims of education serves as a primary consideration. Partnerships can actually help us to move the discussion of adult learning out of the academy and into the offices of company personnel responsible for human resource development, government officials charged with the promotion of worker education and training, and union representatives who work on training, enrichment, and general education programs.

Keep Your Options Open

Knowing when the partnership has run its course can be difficult to determine. The decision will often be made for you when you reach the end of the contract and renegotiation is not an option. However, it is not uncommon for a successful project to be discontinued simply because the foundation for continuation was not prepared in advance. It is often difficult to talk about forging a new relationship or continuing the existing one during the term of the present relationship. Nevertheless, in the final months or years of the contract period (depending on the budget cycle), discussions of the day-to-day operation of the project need to be supplemented by conversations about the feasibility of continuing the relationship. This often means talking informally to union officials, company staff, or your counterparts at other colleges to sound them out. There is no blueprint for this discussion and the path to renegotiation is typically more art than science. The direction that adult education policy takes over the course of a legislative session may also influence the prospects for the continuation of partnerships. But these contingencies should not dissuade you from formulating a strategy as early as possible.

Conclusion

As the educational needs of adult learners continue to expand and diversify, strategic partnerships will become increasingly common and important. I have highlighted a set of issues that can lead to the development of best practice strategies for choosing and maintaining partnerships that are right for your institution. In summary, they are:

- Know your institutional life cycle(s).

- Stay focused on your goals for the partnership.

- Make the partnership serve the university, not the other way around.

- Monitor communication loops continuously.

- Use the partnership to strengthen and reinvigorate the adult education mission.

- Draw from creative partnerships to reinvent the university.

- Determine the right number of partners for your project.

- Recognize that partnerships can alter the way your partner values adult education.

- Develop a continuation plan or an exit strategy during the life of the project.

References

Arnone, M. (2002, June 28). International consortium readies ambitious distance-education effort. *Chronicle of Higher Education,* p. A28.

Aronowitz, S. (2000). *The knowledge factory: Dismantling the corporate university and creating true higher learning.* Boston, MA: Beacon Press.

Duderstadt, J. J. (1997–1998). Transforming the university to serve the digital age. *Cause/Effect, 20*(4), 21–32.

Eurich, N. P. (1990). *The learning industry: Education for adult workers.* Princeton, NJ: Carnegie Foundation for the Advancement of Teaching.

Johnson, J. E., & Cooper, G. D. (1999). Corporate universities: What are they and how are they partnering with traditional universities? *Journal of Continuing Higher Education, 47,* 3–8.

Knowles, M. S. (1962). *The adult education movement in the United States.* New York, NY: Holt, Rinehart, & Winston.

Leach, W. (1993). *Land of desire: Merchants, power, and the rise of a new American culture.* New York, NY: Vintage Books.

Martin, J., & Samuels, J. E. (2002, May 17). We were wrong; try partnerships, not mergers. *Chronicle of Higher Education,* p. B10.

Meister, J. C. (2001, February 9). The brave new world of corporate education. *Chronicle of Higher Education,* p. B10.

Miller, R. I. (1999). *Major American higher education issues and challenges in the 21st century.* London, England: Jessica Kingsley.

Paulson, K. (2002, September/October). FIPSE: Thirty years of learning anytime and anywhere. *Change, 34*(5), 36–41.

Pietrykowski, B. (2001). Information technology and commercialization of knowledge: Corporate universities and class dynamics in an era of technological restructuring. *Journal of Economic Issues, 35,* 1–13.

U.S. Department of Education, National Center for Education Statistics. (2003). *Distance education at degree-granting postsecondary institutions: 2000–2001* (NCES 2003–017). Washington, DC: Author. Retrieved September 16, 2004, from http://nces.ed.gov/pubs2003/2003017.pdf

5

Recruiting and Admitting Adult Learners: They're Not Just Older—They're Different

Iris H. Kelsen, Lawrence T. Lesick

At colleges and universities across America, a large number of our students are invisible. They're invisible not because they don't attend class, or because they're not involved in the educational process: Rather, they're invisible because they don't conform to the stereotype of the typical college student who attends full-time immediately after leaving high school, is supported by parents, and may work only part-time if at all. These invisible students are adult learners.

This cohort of adults is of considerable size. In 2000, 39% of all college students were 25 or older and 56% were 22 or older (U.S. Department of Education, 2002). Another way of looking at traditional students is the degree to which they conform to the stereotype of the typical college student mentioned above. Only 27% meet this definition; thus 73% of all undergraduates are nontraditional learners (U.S. Department of Education, 2002). The Council for Adult and Experiential Learning (2000) defines adult learners as financially independent of parents, having major life responsibilities outside of school (such as work, home, or community), and unwilling to identify themselves primarily as students.

Difficulties confront the admission professional because of the invisibility of adult learners within the context of three major orientations. The first comprises federal and state governments and their financial aid policies. Bailey and Mingle (2003) note that while the majority of Pell Grant recipients are independent students, the size of the grant has not kept pace with the increasing costs of education. State aid programs sometimes limit the participation of adult learners. For example, the highly touted Hope Scholarship Program of the state of Georgia requires that high school graduates who do not immediately go to college first complete a year of higher education before they can qualify for the award (Bailey & Mingle, 2003). Furthermore, opportunities for educational loans are typically countered by the fact that adult learners often have other significant financial obligations, such as a mortgage.

A second group that typically does not take adult learners into consideration is the large number of publications that rank colleges and universities. For example, the 2004 edition of the *U.S. News & World Report* annual publication *America's Best Colleges* was geared toward high school students beginning the college application process. Rankings are based on criteria that include academic reputation, SAT or ACT scores of entering freshmen, percentage of faculty who are full-time, and the alumni giving rate. The publication is filled with advice to prospective students on such issues as writing the college application essay, visiting campuses, and getting help from guidance counselors. Nowhere, however, is there any mention of adult students and their efforts to select a college. Similar deficiencies are found in the 2004 edition of *Newsweek's* annual publication *How to Get Into College*. Even though this edition includes a sidebar on "The Changing Face of American Students," it only reports changes in student gender, ethnicity, and ideology—no mention is made of age (Kaplan/Newsweek, 2003, p. 7).

Perhaps most unfortunate is that many of the colleges and universities that serve nontraditional students often treat them as invisible. A lack of flexibility in institutional policies regarding the transfer of courses, class scheduling, academic appeals, and payment options, to name a few, clearly demonstrates the lack of focus on those who do not meet the institutional definition of a college student.

When any combination of these three perspectives doesn't support the existence of nontraditional students, the admission professional is hampered in assisting adult learners to pay for college, identify schools that offer the best fit, and meet the basic educational needs and professional goals that the student brings when he or she is ready to attend college.

There is, however, a mixed but growing body of material to assist professionals in recruiting and admission activities. A search of the ERIC

(Education Resources Information Center) database revealed approximately 200 titles in the last 35 years on recruiting adult students. Hadfield's (2003) article "Recruiting and Retaining Adult Students," as well as numerous pieces in *New Directions for Adult and Continuing Education* and the *Journal of Continuing Higher Education* provide useful guidance. Collections of best practices and works by various organizations are also helpful (e.g., American Council on Education & The Alliance: An Association for Alternative Degree Programs for Adults, 1990; The College Board, 1990; Council for Adult and Experiential Learning, 2000; Flint, Zakos, & Frey, 1999). Professional conferences and organizations provide training and insights into recruiting adults. For example, the Aslanian Group offers two seminars, "The Basics" and "Beyond the Basics," to college and university marketers.

Most major conferences on enrollment management, admission, and recruiting pay very little attention to adult learners. For instance, the 14th annual Strategic Enrollment Management Conference (2002) contained just two sessions on adult learners. The program schedule for the annual meeting of the National Association for College Admission Counseling (2003) showed no sessions devoted to adults and admission. The 14th annual Symposium for the Marketing of Higher Education (2003) offered only two sessions on marketing to adults (one of which was offered by the president of the Aslanian Group).

One annual conference that does focus directly on the recruiting and admission of adult students is the National Conference on the Adult Learner, sponsored by the University of South Carolina, now in its 19th year. The clearest sign, however, that adult students are becoming more visible to the admission profession is the proliferation of consultants who can provide services directed at this market.

In managing an adult recruiting program, there are three issues to consider.

- What does the market look like?

- Does the institution have the programs and services that the market will buy?

- How do you communicate with the market to recruit them to your institution?

The Adult Student Market

Adult learners are typically described as those students who are 25 years and older. Aslanian (2001) notes that 65% of adult learners are women, 88% are white Americans, 66% are married and employed full-time in professional positions, and 70% are part-time students. Many adults receive partial or full tuition reimbursement from their employers to assist with their college education, but increasing numbers of adult learners are also relying on financial aid (primarily loans) to meet their educational expenses. According to Aslanian, the reason most frequently given by adults for deciding to return to college is their career: to retain their current position or to advance to a new one.

The National Center for Education Statistics estimates that there were nearly 6 million college students over the age of 24 in 2000, and these numbers increase if students considered to be "minimally nontraditional" are included (U.S. Department of Education, 2002). Most adult learners attempted college while younger but did not complete their studies for reasons that include lack of commitment leading to poor grades, personal problems, and financial difficulties. When they decide to renew their pursuit of a degree, they bring with them transfer credits from one or more institutions and life experiences that may translate into college credits through experiential learning portfolios, proficiency exams, and other nontraditional methods of credit acquisition.

Programs and Services

Another major factor for this target population is the programs and services offered to adult students. The competition for adult learners is fierce. Not only is there competition from other traditional brick and mortar institutions, but also from distance learning providers, corporate colleges (e.g., Barnes and Noble), proprietary institutions, and noncredit training opportunities. If an institution cannot or will not provide an adult learner with a product that he or she values and in a manner that is acceptable, that student will quickly take his or her business elsewhere. This is the growing consumer nature of the 21st-century adult learner.

For your adult learner program to succeed, you should consider the following.

- *Convenience, convenience, convenience.* Adult learners look for institutions that are conveniently located to their home or office. However, location is not the only important convenience factor for this market. Courses should be offered at times and in formats that fit adults' busy schedules (e.g., accelerated, evenings, weekends, online). All services, including admission, academic and financial aid advising, registration, and bookstore should be available in one location and at times convenient to adults. (Many successful programs refer to this as one-stop shopping.) The application and registration processes should be simple, efficient, and timely, and the ability to perform these processes online is a definite plus. Parking should be plentiful, close to the classrooms, safe, and free of charge.

- *Career-oriented academic programs.* Although many adult learners will state that they "just want to get through as quickly as possible," many employers still insist on a degree that is job related, especially if the employer is funding all or part of the bill. According to Aslanian (2001), the five fields of study most popular with degree-seeking adult learners are business, education, health, engineering, and computer science, so the career connection is obvious.

- *Opportunities for nontraditional acquisition of credits.* Adult learners appreciate the opportunity to demonstrate the knowledge gained from their prior learning experiences and to receive college credit for what they've learned. This validates the importance of the life experiences that they have attained outside the college classroom. The CLEP (College-Level Examination Program), ACE PONSI (Program on Noncollegiate Sponsored Instruction of the American Council on Education), and experiential learning analysis are important services that colleges serving adult learners can offer.

- *Flexible transfer policy.* The last thing an adult learner wants to hear is that previous coursework will not transfer to a prospective institution. Your institution will need to focus special attention on adult learner transfer policies to ensure they are user-friendly without sacrificing academic integrity.

Competition for the adult learner's time also comes from nonacademic sources (e.g., career and family). The admission professional must be able to demonstrate how the institution will enable the adult learner to achieve his or her educational goals as efficiently as possible while mini-mizing the disruption to these other factors. The programs and services included here are critical components in the adult learner's decision to enroll.

Marketing and Communication

Institutional Commitment to Adult Education

Having identified your market and what you have to offer as an institu-tion, your next task is to communicate your services in ways most likely to attract students. First, there are four major points that should be exam-ined: institutional commitment, market research, marketing plan, and the importance of data collection.

Your college or university should determine how nontraditional edu-cation fits within its mission, organizational structure, and budget. For some institutions—and here the University of Phoenix is the exemplar—adult education is the mission. Consequently, issues such as majors of-fered, faculty teaching load, cost and payment issues, and customer service come directly from the institutional focus on the adult learner. For most baccalaureate colleges, however, offering nontraditional programs for adult learners is often something of an afterthought. This is evident by where these programs are located, institutionally. The head of adult learn-ing typically reports to a senior administrator in academic affairs rather than directly to the president. Likewise, adult programs tend to be looked upon more as cash cows and are considered last when doling out expendi-ture budgets. These issues are likely to be even more exaggerated if most of the adult program takes place at off-campus locations. The old adage "out of sight, out of mind" holds particularly true here.

These same kinds of issues are typically prevalent in recruiting new adult students. Is the recruiting of adult learners a part of the overall ad-missions effort? Is there an integrated marketing program that includes adult education? Unfortunately, the recruiting of adults is often an after-thought.

In most cases, adult learner programs are high revenue/low overhead programs. Adult educators have a responsibility to serve as an advocate and make the case for their adult program at their institution. The best way to influence the president, senior staff, and faculty is to have the chief adult educator serve as a senior staff member. Unfortunately, this is rare, but there are other ways to get the attention of decision-makers. The first is to demonstrate, on a regular basis, the level of contribution that the adult programs make to the bottom line. What percentage of tuition revenue do nontraditional students provide? What percentage of net revenue? How does this amount compare to the amount that the advancement office is able to generate each year? Putting revenue into an institutional context can be an especially powerful tool in developing support for recruiting adult students, and in support of adult programs overall.

Another way to get the attention of decision-makers is to compare the cost of recruiting a new adult student to that of a traditional student. Since many colleges focus a disproportionate amount of advertising on nontraditional programs, the argument can also be made that this exposure can benefit traditional programs.

You may wish to demonstrate to the senior administration how new courses, majors, program development, and delivery systems are often implemented by and designed for nontraditional programs. In this application, adult learner programs act, in effect, as "skunk works" or research and development departments, and they provide entrepreneurial ways of doing things that can be transferred to traditional programs once they have proven their worth.

Having said this, you must understand that it is a never-ending task to get and keep the attention of senior staff and faculty in support of recruiting adults. Presidents, in particular, have enormous demands on their time. Adult learner programs—even if they generate a disproportionate amount of the net income—most likely only comprise a small segment of the entire institution's mission and are not likely to be a primary focus. This is typically exacerbated by the fact that most presidents (and faculty, for that matter) were not adult students themselves, so their idea of a typical college student is based on their own "traditional" experience. Your responsibility as adult educators—and especially leaders of adult programs—is to continue to lobby on behalf of your programs. In so doing, you are no different from any other constituency on your college campus.

Market Research

An incredible amount of research is available on the traditional student market, including high school graduation projections, academic programs, and parental income. There are numerous organizations eager to sell colleges and universities the names of prospective students, as well as their test scores, anticipated majors, and interests. Traditional-aged students can be contacted via high school visits or college fairs, long the staples of the standard recruiting process.

Similar data on adult learners, however, is not as easy to come by. One place to start is the National Center for Education Statistics. Another simple and direct type of market research is to canvas your current students. Are they female or male? Where do they work? What is their age? How did they learn about you? What are their goals? Why do they attend your institution rather than another in the area? Even though consultants and advertisers will take on market research tasks, these are very expensive and may be of limited value. You can gain many answers from among the adult population that already exists at your school.

One final source of market research is your own marketing plan. The success of your recruiting in the past can give you ideas about what the market is seeking, what your competitors are doing, and what opportunities are available.

Marketing Plan

The marketing plan has several purposes. The first is to provide an argument for the place of the recruitment of adults within the mission and strategic plan of the institution. You will need to garner support for the plan itself and to raise the profile of adult learning programs. This is part of your internal marketing effort to the president, senior staff, and faculty. Unless you make your case to these internal stakeholders, the plan—and the marketing efforts it contains—will end up on the shelf as just another report.

A second purpose of the marketing plan is to clearly outline budget, timeline, and enrollment goals. This can help you determine your allocation of resources, identify bottlenecks in the process, coordinate the work of your staff, and inform vendors and other offices of your deadlines and needs.

Numerous templates are available for a marketing plan, but the following topics should be included: an executive summary or introduction; a statement of the benefits of your programs (your brand); an analysis of strengths, weaknesses, opportunities, and threats (SWOT analysis); a listing of your recruitment activities, including a timeline; a fairly detailed budget; a statement of what you want the implementation of the plan to achieve; and an explanation of how you will measure the results.

The *executive summary* is just that—a snapshot of the entire plan. It is for the benefit of those (you can read "president and senior staff" here) who want to know how you plan to achieve your goals but may not be as interested in all the details (although you can be assured that the chief financial officer or budget director will be particularly interested in your budget).

If you plan to market a service, you should be very clear about the *benefits* of that service. You will need to put together a cogent statement of the bundle of benefits that your institution can provide, and explain how it meets the needs of your market better than your competition. Sevier (1998) calls these your "vivid descriptors" or your "points of pride" (p. 80). Do you have any unique academic programs? Do you offer your programs in unique ways ? Is your institutional heritage of any advantage to the adult learner? One thing to remember is that your "points of pride" should be of interest to your market, not just to you. For instance, very few prospective students, and fewer adult students overall, care when your college was founded, but learning that you offer free, convenient parking may help in their final decision!

The *SWOT analysis* is a standard tool of marketers. Analyzing your strengths, weaknesses, opportunities, and threats allows you to examine the landscape of the market (external) and your place in it (internal). The environmental scan will be of particular importance. This should include an assessment of the economy, government regulations, business policies in support of higher education, and an evaluation of your competition. The SWOT analysis should be fairly short, about three to five points for each of the four topics. You should also be brutally honest and realistic. If a lack of customer service to your adult learners is a weakness, state that and then look to it as an opportunity for improvement. Do not allow your president or faculty to sugarcoat weaknesses or threats. At the same time, you should keep yourself and others from dwelling on the barriers to success, since this can ultimately lead to paralysis.

The largest section of your plan will be the listing of your *recruitment activities.* These should be specific, be part of a timeline, identify the person(s) responsible for their completion, and include a budget and the method of evaluating the success of the activity. The activities should include all of the following.

Building and maintaining a list of prospects. Adult learners drop in and out of the educational process at a significantly greater rate than their traditional classmates. It is important to include students who have "stopped out" on the prospect list as well as those who have not yet attended your institution. Also, while it is important to cull your list periodically, an adult prospect may warrant a longer stay on a list than a traditional prospect. That's because it is more likely that the latter individual chose another institution, whereas the former may have just deferred the start of his or her program.

Advertising with radio, television, in print, and billboards. Market research may help you determine which source of advertising produces the highest yield rates for your population. Radio ads during the morning and evening commute time are generally a good source of prospects. Other types of advertising should be used to establish your brand, to provide your prospects with an awareness of who you are, and to directly market to them. Avoid cutting back on brand-building advertising just because it does not produce immediate results. According to Sevier (2002), "prospective students have to be aware of you before they can determine if what you offer will benefit them" (p. 88).

Communicating electronically. Make it easy for your prospective students to communicate with you via email. Virtually everyone who works in an office setting has a computer, so make certain you collect email addresses. If you plan to do mass emails, make certain that you get your prospects' permission and give them an easy way to opt out. Your web site should be adult friendly; all of your advertising should direct adults to a special catch page on your institution's web site, not just its main page. At the least, adults should be specifically directed to the location that will best serve their needs. If you plan to give your students electronic access to your system, do so without requiring them to install special software on their computers, since employers are likely to prohibit this practice.

Direct mail. In addition to sending materials to prospective students who are already on your list of prospects, you can purchase names of prospects from numerous list brokers. Do not just buy the names of people at every address in your service area. Limit your list to those whose demographics resemble those students you already have enrolled. Johnson (1999) advises schools to canvas their current students' magazine reading habits and then buy the names of people in their area who subscribe to those magazines. Publications do not need to be high gloss with numerous campus photographs. They should contain relevant information such as descriptions of programs, costs, courses, the process for admission and registration, and outcomes for adult graduates. Photographs should show adult students in class so that prospects will know they will not be lost in a group of 18- to 22-year-olds.

Open houses and information sessions. These direct-contact opportunities should be held at times convenient for adult learners. They should be short and to the point, focusing on the programs and services that you offer to adults and that differentiate you from your competition. Make current students available during your information sessions to answer questions from the student perspective.

Yield activities. The adult recruiting cycle from inquiry to registration is often very short, so you probably will not have enough time to implement a series of yield activities. The most common and effective type may simply be a phone call or email after a prospective student has requested information. The content of these messages can be as simple as an offer to provide more information or answer questions. The message can also be used to reinforce the student's decision to continue his or her education.

Outreach to employers. Contacting employers, especially those that have current students who are employees, can help identify other students and needs that the employer may have. Setting up a table in the employer's cafeteria or providing a mini-information session at lunchtime is good, but many employers are wary of participation by only one institution. It is more effective to form a consortium of local colleges and universities to provide "college fairs" at the employer's location. Another effective means of employer outreach is the establishment of an advisory board. Besides providing you with valuable input about your courses and programs, members of an advisory board can also provide their employees with information about your institution.

There is often some discussion about how much *budget* is enough. The truth is that there is never enough money to cover everything you want to accomplish! That's the case not only in recruiting but in any area of the institution. Much of your success depends on where you spend your limited dollars. One institution spends $75,000 on advertising and has five admission staff members to recruit students. Another, in the same state, spends $130,000 on advertising, yet has only one and one-half recruiters. Which one is right? That depends.

The only satisfactory way to determine whether a budget is adequate is to answer the following questions: Did the resources allocated enable you to achieve your enrollment goals? What are your competitors or benchmark schools spending? There is no simple answer associated with either of these questions. Your response to the first question assumes that you spent your budget wisely. There will always be those who claim that you did not. The answer to the second question depends on the willingness of your competitors to tell you how much they spend to recruit their students. Since this information may not always be forthcoming, you can reach an approximation. If you find that you're competing with XYZ University and both of you are offering the same programs at the same price, you can get some sense of your competitor's budget by talking to its representatives and monitoring its advertising before making simple comparisons with your own budget.

Data collection for potential and current adult learners is critical, but a good database of such information does not always exist. One reason may be that the traditional database was in existence long before the need to capture information on nontraditional students arose, and the relevant fields are not in the system. Another may be that the data collectors for traditional and nontraditional programs are different staffs in geographically different locations, and they do not work together to maximize the efficiencies of the system. At a minimum, the following information should be captured (Dehne, n.d.):

- Name
- Address
- Home telephone number
- Program or programs of interest
- Educational background
- Name of employer
- Third-party payee
- Desired enrollment date
- Work telephone number

Once the above information is collected and entered into the database, it is important to manage the database with respect to two key items that relate more specifically to adult learners: length of time from inquiry to enrollment and stop outs.

According to Dehne (n.d.), it may take several years from a nontraditional student's first inquiry to his or her enrollment in your program. It is important that you keep in contact with this person throughout this period and that you do not remove his or her name from your mailing list until it is obvious that the person is no longer a prospect.

Once an adult learner enrolls in your institution, that student may periodically stop out for one, two, or more semesters due to competing factors in the student's personal or professional life. Remaining in contact with these students is especially important so that you can encourage them to return. Therefore, it is crucial to maintain accurate data on these stop out students.

There should be an institution-wide approach to data collection, maintenance, and retention. If there are separate staffs dealing with these issues at separate locations, they should periodically meet to share processes. If the institution employs an institutional researcher, he or she should be held accountable for providing information for *all* students in *all* programs and locations. Information technology is crucial to understanding and serving your students. Schools that invest wisely in this tool will enhance their chances of success. Information technology is probably the best way to assess how well you are doing and which areas need greater attention.

Lessons Learned

- The recruitment of adults is at least as competitive as it is for traditional students. Some might argue that it is *more* competitive because of the expansion of for-profit and corporate schools that offer both distance and classroom learning. To remain competitive in this environment, colleges must continually evaluate their message, marketing efforts, and academic program offerings.

- Schools must provide adequate resources to support adult learner programs. One major benefit is that these programs can serve as beta sites or "skunk works" and develop programs or procedures that can benefit all students.

- Although this should be self-evident, it bears repeating: Adult learners are different from traditional students and must be treated as such. Focus on their needs and, when in doubt, *ask them.* Institutions must segment their markets, pay attention to their customers, and provide the services, aligned with the institutional mission, that their customers require.

- A sea change will have to occur before adult learners become central to the academy. Until then, understand that professionals in this area perform a vital service that is important to a significant group of students and that is important to your institution in terms of enrollment, use of resources, and net revenue.

- It is your responsibility to keep nontraditional education on the agenda of the senior staff, especially the president, chief academic officer, and chief financial officer. Provide them with national and institutional data, pass along articles from newspapers, arrange opportunities for them to meet with nontraditional students, and stress the benefits that accrue to the institution because of adult programs.

- Recognize that however difficult your job, your potential market is enormous. Unlike the recruiters for the 18-year-old market (which changes every year), recruiters for adult learners can look at their market as being anyone over the age of 25 who does not have their degree. And you can keep going back to recruit that nontraditional student until he or she enrolls.

- You will *never* have enough time, staff, or money. Your task is to use the resources you have as efficiently and productively as possible.

- Enjoy yourself. You get to work in one of the most intellectually stimulating environments in the academy. You provide a service that virtually everyone appreciates and believes in. Furthermore, you get to see the dramatic difference that education makes in the lives of your students.

References

American Council on Education & The Alliance: An Association for Alternative Degree Programs for Adults. (1990). *Principles of good practice for alternative and external degree programs for adults.* Washington, DC: American Council on Education. Retrieved September 15, 2004, from http://www.ahea .org/pogp.htm

Aslanian, C. B. (2001). *Adult students today.* New York, NY: The College Board.

Bailey, A. A., & Mingle, J. R. (2003). *The adult learning gap: Why states need to change their policies toward adult learners.* Denver, CO: Education Commission of the States. Retrieved September 17, 2004, from http://www.ecs.org/clearinghouse/47/86/4786.pdf

The College Board, Office of Adult Learning Services. (1990). *100 ways colleges serve adults.* New York, NY: Author.

Council for Adult and Experiential Learning. (2000). *Serving adult learners in higher education: Principles of effectiveness* (Executive summary). Chicago, IL: Author. Retrieved September 15, 2004, from http://www.cael.org/alfi/PDF%20files/Summary%20of%20Alfi%20 Principles%20of%20Effectiveness.pdf

Dehne, G. C. (n.d.). *Attracting adult students.* Retrieved November 1, 2003, from http://www.dehne.com/news_research/research_attracting _adults.html

Flint, T. A., Zakos, P., & Frey, R. (1999). *Best practices in adult learning: A self-evaluation workbook for colleges and universities.* Chicago, IL: Council for Adult and Experiential Learning.

Hadfield, J. (2003). Recruiting and retaining adult students. In D. Kilgore & P. J. Rice (Eds.), *New directions for student services: No. 102. Meeting the special needs of adult students* (pp. 17–25). New York, NY: Wiley.

Johnson, R. E. (1999). More than direct mail: Developing a direct marketing strategy. In R. A. Sevier & R. E. Johnson (Eds.), *Integrated marketing communication: A practical guide to developing comprehensive communication strategies* (pp. 211–238). Washington, DC: Council for Advancement and Support of Education.

Kaplan/Newsweek. (2003). The changing face of American students. *How to Get Into College, 2004 Edition,* p. 7.

Sevier, R. A. (1998). *Integrated marketing for colleges, universities, and schools: A step by step planning guide.* Washington, DC: Council for Advancement and Support of Education.

Sevier, R. A. (2002). *Building a brand that matters: Helping colleges and universities capitalize on the four essential elements of a block-buster brand.* Hiawatha, IA: Strategy.

U. S. Department of Education, National Center for Education Statistics. (2002). *Nontraditional undergraduates* (NCES 2002–012). Washington, DC: Author. Retrieved September 16, 2004, from http://nces.ed.gov/pubs2002/2002012.pdf

6

Adult Learner Advising: The Vital Link

Sue Grunau

Academic advisors have long known what college presidents and other policymakers are only now learning: There is a significant correlation between quality advising, student satisfaction, enhanced persistence, and graduation. "Good advising may be the single most underestimated characteristic of a successful college experience" (Light, 2001, p. 81).

Academic advising, particularly for adult students, has often been relegated to a secondary position in the larger scheme of academic services. This chapter focuses on adult advising services by:

- Understanding the unique aspects of advising adult students

- Examining the advisor/advisee relationship

- Exploring best practices for advising adults in a variety of educational settings

Since advising adults is multidimensional and can be as unique as the advisor and the institution that employs the advisor, a portion of this chapter will be dedicated to the experiences and insights shared by representatives from four different institutions: K. Page Boyer, Harvard Business School; Gary Carr, University of Toledo; Gina Cuffari, University of Phoenix–Ohio Campus; Joel Martin, Chemeketa Community College. I am indebted to them for their expertise, their professionalism, and their willingness to supply substantive information. Their participation has contributed immeasurably to the content of this chapter.

Unique Aspects of Advising Adults

The roots of academic advising can be traced as far back as 1877, when Johns Hopkins University initiated a formal faculty-based advising system (Kramer, 1995). Early advising for academics was fairly straightforward and geared to students of traditional age. In those days, faculty informed students which courses would meet graduation requirements, and students registered into and completed those courses.

Advising is now seen as a decision-making process engaged in by the advisor and the student. Kramer (1995) describes academic advising as a process that is "ongoing, multifaceted, and the responsibility of both student and advisor" (p. 3). The relationship between advisor and advisee is seen as "shared responsibility," a term that appears with increasing frequency in the advising literature (Frost, 1991). This movement toward a more collaborative approach to advising has special significance for the advising of adult learners.

An assumption exists that adults come to the academy with a chosen program of study and plan to complete that program and reach their academic goals. Those of us engaged in advising adults find that frequently the opposite is true. There are isolated instances when employment or personal circumstances dictate an adult's course of study, but very often we find that adults need assistance in choosing appropriate majors and selecting courses and course delivery options. They frequently request help in sequencing coursework and planning schedules. Successful advising for adults requires a delicate balance between providing guidance and information and honoring the adult learner's need to be an integral part of the planning process.

Adults expect advisors to be knowledgeable in multiple areas. They demand specific information regarding courses and course instructors, including course workloads and instructor personality profiles. Adults will often ask if a professor exhibits a level of understanding and appreciation of what it takes to be an adult learner. Adults will usually articulate their desire to have coursework be meaningful and applicable in their daily lives.

Adults turn to advisors for information on how program requirements will fit with the advisee's ultimate life or career goals. Many adults return to school to find new options for future employment or to discover ways to supplement knowledge in their current career fields. The wise advisor will be prepared with resource information and contact persons for the student's follow-up.

Adult learners tend to be highly motivated and concerned about their academic performance. Work and family responsibilities impact adult students' abilities to advocate for themselves. The discerning advisor arms students with appropriate knowledge of policies and procedures and encourages them to be proactive in dealing with performance issues.

Advising for the adult learner demands recognition of the multiplicity of life situations that can affect attendance, academic performance, and well-being. Adults may disclose personal problems during an academic advising session. The astute advisor knows that these situations demand intervention by other professionals qualified to handle specific problems and will refer a student to an appropriate person or organization. Knowing when to differentiate between academic advising and personal counseling affirms the advisor's professionalism and respect for confidentiality.

The Advisor/Advisee Relationship

Many adults return to school during the third and fourth decades of life. Researchers and developmental theorists see this period as one of instability brought about by an emotional awareness of one's own mortality. Life choices are reassessed. New searches for meaning surface. Women, especially, begin reaching out in new directions, abandoning old roles and seeking new opportunities (Robinson, 1979).

Advisors of adult learners need to be particularly sensitive to this critical stage of life development. Contributors to this chapter affirm the need to understand the insecurities that are often present in undertaking a new and frightening experience at this stage of adult life.

- One of the first big issues adult learners face is lack of confidence in school (Martin, Chemeketa Community College)

- Adult students' concerns may often be based in fear (Cuffari, University of Phoenix)

- Adults are often reluctant to acknowledge that they need help and are unsure about how to ask for it (Boyer, Harvard Business School)

- Advisors need to reinforce the "better student" aspect of adult students. Adults are more focused and have better time management skills, even though they may not recognize these qualities (Martin, Chemeketa Community College)

- Adults often have previous college or school experiences which were less than successful (Cuffari, University of Phoenix)

Literature corroborates:

- Adults come to the academy with a full set of baggage: responsibilities, inhibitions, reservations, time constraints, anxieties, and sometimes, even a sense of fear (Robinson, 1979)

- Adults are often affected by situation phenomena: job or health problems, financial problems, legal problems, family or personal problems (Wonacott, 2001)

- Adults play multiples roles and often are experiencing some sort of life transition at the time they decide to return to school (Skorupa, 2002)

- Adults often need help in juggling all their varied commitments (Bailey, 2003)

Bash (2003) offers additional insight:

- Adults come to the academy with a strong sense of urgency and high motivation

- Adults come to the college experience with unique sets of expectations

- Adults come to the academy with individual approaches to learning

- Adults are intrinsically motivated, task- and problem-centered rather than subject-centered

- Adults have a deep need to be self-directing (Bash, 2003)

It is impossible to overemphasize the critical nature of the advisor/advisee relationship. Early rapport established through person-to-person connections (whether they be via email, telephone, or in person) sets the tone for future communication. The perceptive advisor recognizes how a positive first encounter influences all ensuing contacts. Feedback indicates that adult students seek availability and competence in an advising situation.

They want an advisor to recognize their unique needs and address those needs with efficiency, intelligent feedback, expertise, and sensitivity.

Advisors in the academy of the 21st century must also deal with the impact of technology. No longer relegated to the in-person office visit, advising often takes place via email, telephone, online chat groups, and even teleconferences. Web sites provide a broad spectrum of information that allows students to do everything from comparison shopping for institutional fit to enrollment and admission. Electronic communication helps busy adults obtain answers to simple questions. Advisors who fail to adapt or find new ways to enhance contact with advisees compromise the effectiveness of the advisor/advisee relationship.

Capella University develops a rapport with new online students by using a three-person team and a "New Learner Webboard." Two members of the team make the initial enrollment contact, taking the prospective student through the enrollment and admission steps. Once the new learner's file is complete it is turned over to his or her academic advisor, who makes contact with the student. The advisor encourages registration in online courses. A user name and password is then assigned to the student for access to the New Learner Webboard. Subsequently, the registered student is encouraged to participate in discussions, post questions, search the library, or just chat with other learners. The three members of the enrollment and advising team post announcements and monitor the webboard discussions in order to respond to questions (Maday, 2001).

The continuing emergence of advising using electronic means will result in new challenges and choices. Advisors will discover tools of technology that will help make the best and most current information available to advisees. Advisors and advisees will communicate more frequently by electronic means, and advisors who embrace technology will find new ways to improve the advising relationship.

Making Adult Advising Work: Best Practices in the Academy

As advisors of adults in the academy, we commit time, energy, and money to the improvement of services. We spend uncounted hours gleaning from the latest research, selecting and individualizing those pieces particularly applicable to our students and our advising situations. A vast body of knowledge generated through the collective experiences of advisors in the field provides some of the richest available resources. The following contributions represent exemplary practices that are worthy of consideration and replication.

Chemeketa Community College

Joel Martin of Chemeketa Community College has learned in more than 20 years of advising that his work is highly individualized and is often a mix of advising and counseling. One of his favorite questions for adult students is, "How will you know when you know what it is you want to do?" He states this question as a launching pad for the thought processes that accompany the idea of advanced planning. The question is often posed to those students who are coming back to college life after a period of time in the work force. Frequently they have not settled on a major field of study, or are still exploring options. Many adults feel they are "too old" to be back in school, or are unsure of their ability to keep up with the younger students.

Martin finds that many of his adult learners who are returning to school are facing an underlying problem of "painful experiences." He cites such things as supercritical parents and/or teachers, no rewards for good performances or improvement, and negative comments and criticism on poor performance. Martin often suggests a preparatory course for these students to build their academic confidence (see Chapter 7).

The establishment of an online advising system is an innovative outgrowth of the use of technology at Chemeketa Community College. Since the school is one of seventeen institutions in the Oregon Community College System, Martin and a colleague recognized the need for a cooperative effort to coordinate information. An online advising system was launched in the fall of 1999. Here is how it works:

1) A student logs on to the Oregon Community Colleges web site.

2) The prospective student chooses from a variety of options to receive information specific to his or her situation or request.

3) The system sends an automatic message to the college(s).

4) The college responds to the student's online request.

As the person responsible for responding to the requests coming to Chemeketa, Martin feels that one of the great benefits of electronic advising is the ability to embed links to other Chemeketa web site pages in his replies to students. He also feels that each reply deserves a personalized response. He abandoned an earlier option of using boilerplate paragraphs because he found it to be less individualized and less efficient. As Martin provides students with current links, he finds an added benefit in the need to stay current on the college's web site content.

University of Toledo Distance Learning Program
The University of Toledo (U of T) has a distance learning program that has rocketed from no students, courses, or facilities in 1997 to an enrollment of more than 3,200 students in more than 13,000 course enrollments in spring 2003. The program is housed in a state-of-the-art facility in downtown Toledo (see Chapter 10).

Gary Carr, interim director of student services for the U of T distance learning degree program, commented on the range of advising services for this high number of online adult students. A system called TRAX is used to input data for all incoming inquiries. A staff member reviews this data and follows up with each prospective student within 24 hours of an inquiry. Initial advising is provided by the student services staff and consists of assistance with technical problems, admission and registration procedures, adding and dropping of courses, and referrals to appropriate offices and departments. Specific questions regarding academic programs, course choices, and course information are referred to the appropriate department or faculty person.

Advising students in the U of T's distance learning program presents a unique set of challenges. Meeting the needs of students without the benefit of face-to-face conversation dictates creative interventions.

Carr notes that U of T's adult students are more time conscious and demanding of excellent customer service than the traditional age undergraduate. He recognizes the burden of time and financial constraints placed upon adult students. There is a heightened awareness that adult students often lack familiarity with today's technology. Students who have been removed from an educational environment for a longer period of time may be at special risk for the problems associated with lower-level computer skills. With high tech computer skills a necessity for success in a distance learning program, the Division of Distance Learning at U of T sees its role as being a strong student advocate and referral source. A guide for online learners has been developed. Help desk access for technology problems and to access the advising staff for program issues has been extended to evening and weekend hours. A thorough knowledge of campus services and departments is demanded from the staff members in the division, and the targeted turnaround time for responses to student inquiries is less than 24 hours.

U of T has implemented a virtual advising pilot program that uses cameras to converse with program advisors at community colleges where articulation agreements exist. Eventually U of T hopes to use the same equipment and technology to converse with students, which will eliminate the need for on-campus advising visits.

Harvard Business School

K. Page Boyer, director of research staff services in the Harvard Business School (HBS) offers the following insights into adult student advising services at HBS.

The graduate business division at Harvard employs a case method learning model. The need for each student to play an active role, both as teacher and learner, forms an integral piece of this model. Students are charged with enhancing the learning of their section mates, and 50% of the student's grade is based on the quality and frequency of oral class participation. This mandate for class participation and the attendant student attributes needed to compete in a fast-paced, highly intellectual academic environment are the primary factors influencing the necessity for academic advising at HBS.

Students who have come from culturally diverse situations, or environments where pedantic learning is the norm, find themselves faced with enormous challenges when faced with this model. Consider the diversity of the student body at HBS, where 33% are women, 19% are minorities, and 33% are international. There are approximately 70 countries represented in each Harvard class. As Boyer states: "There are enormous cultural and psychological barriers to overcome in helping certain students learn how to learn at HBS."

Boyer enlightens our understanding by providing a sampling of some of the cultural obstacles faced by international students.

- Asian students see the HBS learning model as counterintuitive. Boyer quotes many of her Asian students as saying, "Much talk is the sign of a fool." It is a huge task for these students to overcome the dictates of a culture that requires a student to sit humbly and quietly absorb what is prescribed by the teacher.

- Women in India are considered unfeminine if they are overly verbal.

- Due to language constraints, nonnative English speakers find the fast-paced verbal environment challenging.

The underlying issues of academic advising at HBS often relate to issues of self-esteem rather than academic content. Advising for these students revolves more around the *process* of learning than the content.

Advising practices at HBS consist of a "destigmatization" process that:

- helps students understand how to be more forceful as class participants

- helps students track participation, their own and that of other class members

- provides students with tangible means to attack the public speaking issue through documentation of their own progress and observation of others' participation

- has students obtain feedback from faculty

- assists students in recognizing fears, obstacles, and barriers

- assists students in accepting that doing more of the same (i.e., note taking, reading, analyzing, etc.) will not fix the problem

- helps students recognize that they are not alone and that they are struggling due to the unique aspects of the HBS learning model, not because of a lack of intellectual prowess or suitability.

Coincidentally, an effective means of dealing with the trauma experienced by the HBS advisees is the advisor's sense of humor. Students, who sometimes characterize the academic difficulties they experience as a black hole, can often be helped to put things in perspective by appreciating the lighter side of their dilemma. From reminders of their not-so-isolated predicament ("you are one in a long and distinguished line of students with whom I have had the privilege of working") to illustrations garnered from television comedy, the advisor works to promote a fresh look at the situation.

Students who persevere and turn initially debilitating experiences into positive learning outcomes often communicate the benefits of learning about themselves. They reassess and expand their values. Most importantly perhaps, they improve their ability to overcome perceived inadequacies and fears.

University of Phoenix, Cleveland–Ohio Campus

Gina Cuffari, director of student and financial services, was promoted from an advisory position at the University of Phoenix (UOP) campus in Cleveland. Her perspective on advising students at this highly visible university is a blend of both her old and new roles.

The UOP program consists of placing students in cohort groups and then subgrouping them into smaller parts called learning teams. This somewhat unique approach brings rewards and challenges to advisors working with the students. Students often find the learning team approach to be their favorite aspects of the UOP program. Lifelong friendships ensue. However, challenges may appear as students find that a learning team does not work as a cohesive unit. Advising helps students refocus on their goals and remember that all adult students face challenges at one time or another. The advising approach at UOP centers on problem solving. Reconstructing a student's original motivation for returning to school can often make the difference in dealing with difficulties.

Advisors at the UOP are student centered and customer driven. Many are former or current UOP students. They strive to be experts, not only regarding degree programs, but also concerning policy and procedures. The advising program is unique and special, Cuffari says, because it is focused on the student as a customer first and foremost.

A recent revision in the advising program at the Cleveland campus has combined academic advising and financial aid. UOP cross-trained their advisors over several months and taught them to counsel on both academics and finances. Student feedback provided the impetus for this effort. Cuffari is proud to say that many UOP campuses worldwide are considering this method of advisement.

Several proactive elements of the UOP advising program deserve mention.

- Students are regularly contacted by advisors via email or telephone, providing support and encouragement.

- Routine reminders are sent to students to remind them of their degree requirements.

- Academic progress is monitored through UOP's Department of Institutional Research. Cuffari states "We make our students 'know' what we expect them to know."

- UOP has an ongoing program of assessment that uses surveys to get student feedback on their academic experience and the quality of advising services.

- Advisors base student scheduling on each student's program needs.

Baldwin-Wallace College

Baldwin-Wallace College (B-W) has had an active adult degree program since 1947. The Evening/Weekend College was established as a way to provide higher education to a growing number of adults who wished to return to college. The GI Bill provided a financial impetus for many of these returning students. In addition, women were finding their way into the workforce in ever increasing numbers and were recognizing the need for higher education to augment their career goals.

As the program population grew, advising services were added on an as-needed basis. But a more cohesive response for advising adults became necessary, and in 2001 the advising specialist position was created to address that vision.

A number of factors prompted the revision of the advising program for adult students at B-W.

- A conviction that quality academic advising is not only a privilege but a right that should be extended to all students, including adults

- The existence of increased opportunities for participation in education programs (e.g., certificate programs and additional majors)

- Increased numbers of students coming to the college with transfer credits and life and work experiences

- A desire to know more about the adult student population in order to provide the services it required

- A significant number of adult students who were requesting advising services

After careful consideration, the decision was made in early 2002 to initiate a caseload advising system for the lifelong learning students. There were several factors favoring the anticipated success of the system.

- An accommodating support staff, under cooperative leadership, was available to launch the system.

- B-W had a number of strong professional staff members willing to participate as advisors in the new advising system.

- An adult population of 750–800 students during academic year 2002–2003 provided a relatively manageable number of students to advise.

A number of challenges surfaced while launching the new endeavor.

- How would the advising caseloads be structured?

- How/when would advisors be reimbursed?

- What were the expectations for the advisors?

- What training was necessary?

- What were the implications for the students?

- How should students be incorporated into the changeover?

- How could we determine if caseload advising was effective? What determinants or measurements should be defined?

- How could we control the student information in a comprehensive filing system that had been in place for many years?

- How would the flow of information be handled?

- Who would accept the various roles and responsibilities associated with implementing the new system?

- How could we evaluate the efforts of our advisors?

Student service was the tenet of the revised program and formed its core. Dedication to this principle was the foundation for each decision. As such, caseload advising was envisioned as a way to:

- Provide our adult students with consistency and continuity by connecting them with one advisor who works with them throughout their B-W experience.

- Help the student stay on track to ensure that, as graduation approaches, there are no surprises regarding program completion.

- Give students a sense of connectedness with the institution so they don't feel that college is just a place to attend class.

- Provide synthesis for our adult students among the many elements of life on a college campus. With the majority of the B-W student body comprised of traditional full-time day students, the Division of Lifelong Learning is keenly aware of the need for adults to be comfortable in this environment.

- Link the student, through a personal contact, to the multiple resources and opportunities on the B-W campus. This person-to-person element is, for all intents and purposes, the most vital piece of the caseload advising program philosophy.

The first step in the initiation of caseload advising was to enlist the cooperation and support of the faculty and staff who had been involved with the previous system. One-on-one interviews were conducted with every faculty and staff person who had provided adult advising services in the past. The willingness of each of these persons to supply rich and varied responses to my questions served as a springboard for future actions.

- A decision was made to launch the project with a pilot program encompassing one academic year.

- Three of the advisors who had been working with our students were retained. One new advisor was added.

- The previous hard copy student filing system was retained but new electronic documentation was added. The goal was to eliminate hard-copy documentation of advising notes.

- A computer system training package for advisors was developed by the informational technology staff and a hands-on training session was held.

- All caseload advisors attended an orientation meeting.

As we moved through the early stages of implementation, administrator responsibilities became more clearly defined. For example, caseloads are in a constant state of flux due to the normal patterns associated with college attendance for adults. Advisors are given the responsibility to inform the program administrator when these changes occur. Spreadsheets, developed to track advisor caseloads, are updated in response to these notifications.

Student awareness occupied a preferential place in the plans. A letter of introduction and explanation was written and mailed to each student who would be affected by the caseload advising pilot project. Options were outlined in the event that students might choose not to participate.

Advisor responsibilities also took shape.

- Each advisor maintains a caseload of 30–40 students. As students graduate, stop out, leave the program, or return to the college, advisors notify the administrator for updated advisee assignment.

- Each student on an advisor's caseload is contacted at least once each semester.

- The first advisor contact with a student is expected to be an in-person appointment.

- A checklist for each student is completed at the first advising appointment. This checklist was developed to ensure that the student has firsthand knowledge of important policies, procedures, and program requirements.

- Students with little or no college, at-risk transfer students, or students who have been out of college for more than two years, are encouraged to attend a two-credit "transformation" course designed by the dean of the Division of Lifelong Learning (see Chapter 7).

- Advisors complete an end-of-semester report that documents student contacts, registrations, and other pertinent information.

When the caseload advising system was implemented at B-W, it became apparent after the first semester of reporting that a student contact process needed to be defined. Each advisor was expected to contact each student on his or her caseload at least once each semester. This contact could be made by a phone call, an email message, a letter or postcard, or in person. Advisors reported that some students assigned to their caseloads were difficult or impossible to reach. Knowing that adult students often experience life changes that require them to stop out for indeterminate periods of time, each advisor is now asked to make an initial attempt to contact each student via telephone or email. If no response is received, a second attempt is made. A letter or postcard is used in a third attempt. In some cases, the phone call will provide the information that a number is no longer functioning, or the letter or postcard will be returned, indicating that a student is no longer at that mailing address. This provides valuable information for moving a student to an inactive status and allows the caseload to be adjusted accordingly.

The development of an evaluation tool to enable students to express their opinions regarding this new system is envisioned for future semesters. Using this tool, and the anecdotal feedback from advisors and students, it is expected that we will be able to better define our students and their patterns of retention and satisfaction.

Lessons Learned

Change Requires Coordination and Cooperation

Initiating a new program with extended parameters and responsibilities can only be seen as a challenge. An unforgiving piece of that challenge is the change that must inevitably be a part of the process. Beginning the project without a sense of the institution's culture and history would have been difficult. The initial interviews with past advisors and support persons were critical to the ultimate formation of the program's parameters.

Any venture, whether a revision of an old system, or initiation of a new one, requires coordination and cooperation. Updating the advising system at B-W meant taking a close look at what had gone before, identifying the resources available for implementation, and organizing a structured approach to making the changes necessary for the transition to the new caseload advising system. Although it was apparent that the old advising system needed renovation, instituting a new system required significant changes. Change implies a level of stress for all parties involved. Sensitivity to the impact of those changes is crucial.

Know That Change Will Take Time

Change often takes time, regardless of the desire for immediate implementation. Thoughtful consideration of past practices, identification of project goals, and coordination of a sequence of steps toward accomplishing those goals become a part of the plan. Even well-defined improvements must proceed through the channels of policies and procedures before implementation.

Expect Modifications and Revisions

Some of the best results obtained from implementing a reorganization flow from the involvement of others. The execution of any plan benefits from the suggestions, feedback, and expertise of students, staff, and administration. As the caseload advising plan moved toward fruition, alternate viewpoints emerged. Some of these caused delays and frustrations. A healthy predisposition to the inevitable delays ensured that they did not become obstacles to the plan's completion.

Solicit Guidance and Support From Others

Perhaps the most important lesson learned in bringing any project to fruition is that it does not have to be a solo venture. Seeking advice from people at all levels while organizing ideas, developing goals, and finding ways to meet those goals, helps make the project not only more efficient, but also more meaningful to those involved. A sense of inclusion is critical for everyone involved, especially staff support personnel who may feel that additional duties are imposed without consideration of their impact.

Without the vision and affirmation of the people at the highest levels of administration, no project of this magnitude could be successful. This commitment began at B-W with the vision of the dean of lifelong learning and was supported by all levels of administration including the college president.

Keep a Firm Grip on the Desired Outcome

It is difficult to imagine a caseload advising system that functions efficiently without the leadership of a coordinator. The coordinator holds the pivotal position for collecting, organizing, and applying reliable data, and ultimately for moving the program forward. It is the coordinator's responsibility to see that this ultimate goal stays clearly in focus, since student support and service are the bottom line of any advising venture.

The coordinator's position at B-W is defined as the advising specialist. A repository is needed for assigning advisors to adult students, scheduling appointments, maintaining files, coordinating advisor reports, and overseeing the collection of data. My task as advising specialist involves sorting and organizing this information into a meaningful format to share with other advisors and with the administrative and support staff. An ongoing need exists for refinements and periodic updates. Without coordination, the process could degenerate into disarray.

The fluid nature of advising adults remains a challenge and a concern. Maintaining caseloads is a balancing act, since we know that adults will often come into and go out of an education program. The caseload advising system relies heavily on the constant input of advisors. In a small college, where the advisors for adult students often have multiple responsibilities in addition to advising duties, it is essential for the advising specialist to provide communication flow. Using the college's online Blackboard system to create an exclusive site for the lifelong learning advisors permits instant sharing of announcements, updates, and other pertinent advising information.

Collection of data from advisor reports supports early contentions. Students register earlier which reduces the number of cancelled classes. Students on the advising caseloads show an increased tendency to stay with their programs rather than stopping out. In the long run, the expectation is that students will continue to have better retention records and more positive and consistent advising experiences.

As the pilot program year draws to a close, decisions now loom as to which pieces of the caseload advising program will remain, which must be eliminated, and what revisions and improvements should be made. The encouraging feedback from students and advisors dictates an ongoing commitment to the project and to the adult students at Baldwin-Wallace College.

References

Bailey, C. A. (2003). FAQs: Advising adult learners. *Clearinghouse.* Retrieved March 12, 2004, from http://www.nacada.ksu.edu/clearing house/AdvisingIssues/adultlearnersfaq.htm

Bash, L. (2003). *Adult learners in the academy.* Bolton, MA: Anker.

Frost, S. H. (1991). *Academic advising for student success: A system of shared responsibility* (ASHE-ERIC Higher Education Report No. 3). Washington, DC: George Washington University, Graduate School of Education and Human Development. Retrieved September 17, 2004, from http://www.ericfacility.net/databases/ERIC_Digests/ed340274.html

Kramer, G. L. (1995). Redefining faculty roles for academic advising. In G. L. Kramer (Ed.), *Reaffirming the role of faculty in academic advising* (Monograph Series No. 1, pp. 3–9). Manhattan, KS: National Academic Advising Association. Retrieved March 12, 2004, from http://www.aahe.org/nche/2002/COPs/mentoring/gary_article.pdf

Light, R. J. (2001). *Making the most of college: Students speak their minds.* Cambridge, MA: Harvard University Press.

Maday, T. (2001, Spring). Online academic advising: The Capella model. *Student Affairs On-line, 2,* 2. Retrieved September 20, 2004, from http://www.studentaffairs.com/ejournal/Spring_2001/advising.html

Robinson, R. D. (1979). *Helping adults learn and change.* West Bend, WI: Omnibook.

Skorupa, K. (2002, December). Adult learners as consumers. *Academic Advising News, 25*(3). Retrieved September 20, 2004, from http://www.nacada.ksu.edu/clearinghouse/AdvisingIssues/adultlearners.htm

Wonacott, M. E. (2001). *Adult students: Recruitment and retention* (ERIC Practice Application Brief No. 18). Columbus, OH: Center on Education and Training for Employment. Retrieved March 12, 2004, from http://www.cete.org/acve/docs/pab00027.pdf

7

The Introductory Transformation Course for Adult Learners: Critical and Essential

Lee Bash

While some adult learners may enter a certificate or degree completion program with many years of successful college-level work in their background, others do not have this experience and are overwhelmed by the new environment they face. Best practice institutions often address the special needs of these incoming students with an introductory course that is designed to provide adult learners with tools, skills, and systems that will enable them to succeed.

The challenge for any institution is to create a course that is rigorous yet responsive to the special needs of incoming adult students. The course should be substantial enough to engage adult learners with meaningful college-level tasks. At the same time, it should reflect sensitivity to the distinctive characteristics displayed among inexperienced adult learners. If there is a covert objective for such courses, it is to inspire confidence among the adult learners who successfully complete the class, thus the "transformation." But there is an institutional benefit as well, since these courses consistently demonstrate their ability to increase retention rates among adult learners.

It is hard to imagine the level of fear the typical new adult learner is likely to experience as he or she pursues a degree or certificate in higher education. Since the average adult learner is approximately 38 years old (U.S. Department of Education, 2002), these learners may have been away from a formal classroom for approximately 20 years, though they typically have insights and evidence (often gained from their own children) of the profound changes that have taken place during their absence. In fact, for many of these adult learners, this may be their first collegiate experience, while others may be returning after an unsuccessful first try many years previously. As a result, the anxiety many adult learners experience as they begin their studies is significant and understandable.

Because adults tend to be more sophisticated than younger learners in the manner in which they express themselves—especially in their ability to be guarded when they feel vulnerable—the fear that many adult learners initially experience in the classroom may not be readily noticeable by the instructor. But fear is what most adult learners repeatedly describe when they begin their studies. Many faculty members would be amazed to discover the level of extreme discomfort or anxiety that adult students may be experiencing in their classroom, especially early in the term. Of course, for the students to be willing to discuss this topic, there must be a level of trust and openness that some faculty members don't cultivate or earn. Still—and this can't be emphasized enough—many adult learners report profound levels of fear and apprehension when it comes to new classes, new learning experiences, and the college experience in general.

While some adult learners are able to overcome their anxiety fairly quickly, the intense feelings many other students experience is almost phobic. Without proper support, these feelings may undermine the student's ability to succeed. More adults would probably enroll in college-level courses if they felt reassured that their efforts would be met with compassion, support, and understanding (not to be confused with dilution, reduction of standards, or lack of rigor) by their professors or institution.

Even if many schools or faculty may not recognize how terrified the majority of their incoming adult learners are likely to be, best practice has long recognized the importance of an introductory course designed to provide new adult learners with tools, skills, strategies, and a level of familiarity with what they are about to face. Although such courses may go by different titles, their objectives tend to be similar. Also, they may bring increased retention to the adult program and are likely to support greater student success in the classroom.

These courses tend to be transformative for many of the adult learners who complete them as their initial effort or reentry into higher education. The definition of "transformative learning" offered by Morrell and

O'Connor (2002) suggests that this is precisely what is likely to take place within the context of these introductory courses: "Transformative learning involves experiencing a deep, structural shift in the basic premises of thought, feelings, and actions. It is a shift of consciousness that dramatically and permanently alters our way of being in the world" (p. xvii).

The needs of novice adult learners extend beyond simply minimizing their anxiety. They are perhaps best summarized by Brookfield (1986), who sought to specify criteria for good practice within facilitative adult programs.

> Briefly stated, this critical philosophy regards the facilitation of learning as a value-laden activity in which curricular and programmatic choices reflect normative preferences. It sees adult education as a socialization agent of some force, capable of confirming values and behaviors uncritically assimilated in earlier periods or of prompting adults to challenge the validity of their received ideas and codes.

> *Developing in adults a sense of their personal power and self-worth is seen as a fundamental purpose of all education and training efforts* [italics added]. Only if such a sense of individual empowerment is realized will adults possess the emotional strength to challenge behaviors, values, and beliefs accepted uncritically by a majority. (p. 283)

Therefore, the primary covert objective associated with many entry-level transformation courses is the development of student confidence—a sense of personal power and self-worth gained by the learner. But if this objective serves as a benefit to the adult learner, the programmatic benefits associated with increased retention for the institution tend to justify these courses within a win/win context as well (Bash, Lighty, & Tebrock, 1999). They prepare students with tools and applications they can successfully utilize in the classroom, which also creates an improved learning environment for the instructor.

For example, Ashar and Skenes (1993) determined that social integration played a significant positive role on retention of adult learners, when the class—not the institution—was analyzed. As Kerka (1995) notes about this outcome, "Small groups of peers at the same level of career maturity created a social environment that motivated adult learners to persist" (p. 3). She further notes the following strategies to increase retention. Note how these align perfectly with the typical activities embodied in the initial transformative course for adult learners.

- Preenrollment counseling to establish expectations, give a sense of the university community.

- Personal attention; staff willing to listen; assistance with personal and financial problems.

- Managing the culture of the institution; recognizing adult anxiety about school.

(Kerka, 1995, pp. 4–5)

These activities are consistent with what Chaffee (1998) describes as the caring university. In this environment, she suggests that "We help students succeed in their classes, too, by knowing them, knowing the class requirements, and helping them find a good match and address any deficiencies" (p. 35). She later adds, "We take responsibility for ensuring that they (the students) know our expectations in advance and have a realistic view of their own ability to meet our expectations. We do so in ways that enhance, not undermine, their self-esteem" (p. 36).

Furthermore, Schlossberg, Lynch, and Chickering (1989) confirmed the importance and viability of these entry courses when they examined different formats and successful programs that had presented these courses. They also reinforced the common outcomes: "Opportunities like these help adult learners identify strengths, overcome anxieties, clarify needed resources, and increase their sense of belonging" (p. 79).

General Guidelines and Expectations for Transformation Courses

In a world where degree completion programs likely offer more variety than any other portion of higher education, the expectations associated with transformation courses are equally diverse. First, adult learner programs may offer such courses for noncredit or as a one- or two-credit course. Some programs, such as the University of Phoenix, make the introductory transformation course mandatory for all new students. Such programs are likely to view this course as an opportunity to introduce their adult learners to the foundations that will later define their program and course of study. For other programs, such a course is likely to be optional. These programs depend more on the interests of various students or the course description to drive the enrollment. Of course, some programs fall between these extremes by stipulating a set of specific guidelines that often depend on the previous experiences and background of the new adult learner.

Baldwin-Wallace College (B-W) uses the following criteria to determine which students are encouraged to enroll:

- Any adult student with *less* than a total of 10 hours of credit

- Any adult student seeking admission who has *less* than a 2.3 GPA

- Any adult student who has been out of school *more* than 10 years and has *less* than a 3.0 GPA

Although it is not mandatory that the above students enroll in this course, B-W's Division of Lifelong Learning considers these students *at-risk,* especially if they do not enroll in this course.

Using the B-W Model as an Example

One of the most notable attributes of the B-W course is that *everything* about it is intentional. The way it is formatted, from the advance assignment to the final project (and everything in between), is done with a purpose—though this is apparently seldom obvious to the students.

Before getting into specifics, I want to share some general considerations about my approach to this course.

- *The course is taught at an information overload level.* That is, I don't intend that the students immediately absorb all the details they encounter. What I envision occurs at a student's workplace 2–20 days after the last class meeting. He or she hears an innocent phrase that, on the surface, relates to the workplace. At the same time, it stimulates the student to make a connection about a topic covered earlier during class. Suddenly, it all makes perfect sense—a genuine "aha!" moment. Because each student is required to maintain a journal, many students report this experience happening during the first two weeks after the course is concluded. Others relate similar events happening even later in the term. The purpose of the course is to reinforce an authentic collegiate experience through rigor and exposure to many new ideas.

- *The course is intended to create a sense of security.* By providing an environment that feels safe for the students, the course reinforces the notion that the student is his or her own primary stakeholder. In part, this is accomplished by setting guidelines during the first (critical) 20 minutes of the initial class. For instance, students are encouraged to leave class at any time if they need to use the facilities or respond to any needs (such as getting a cup of coffee). By establishing that they are responsible for themselves they quickly become empowered. They can determine whether leaving—even for a brief period—is in their best interest, rather than seeking "permission." This enables students to assume responsibility for themselves as quickly as possible.

- *The course is brief but intense.* Having tried various scheduling formats, I'm convinced that the most productive schedule for a course such as this is an intense immersion offered the weekend before to the beginning of the term. Our schedule utilizes a Friday afternoon and evening, followed by all-day sessions on Saturday and Sunday so that the course doesn't conflict with the regular classes that begin the following Monday. The schedule enables the students to devote their exclusive attention to the material in the course without the distractions of other assignments or conflicting activities. It also provides many of the students with tools and strategies they can begin to apply immediately in their subsequent courses. Although one of the primary covert objectives of this course—to instill confidence in these novice adult learners—may seem subjective, this outcome is observable and tangible, made more obvious by the intensive nature of the immersion. A special subset of this objective is often obtained shortly after the immersion weekend. Students in the transformation course suddenly find themselves in a new classroom with fellow students they have just shared an intense weekend with. The bonding that takes place as a result of these courses provides informal stability, continuity, and a support system that is often sustained throughout the students' entire enrollment.

- *The course is multidimensional.* Extended periods of time pass quickly when the schedule is broken into shorter segments with different activities assigned to each. Some activities involve focused discussions while others include brief presentations by guest speakers such as a financial aid officer, someone from the learning center, or a person from advising. We also break things up by doing mini fieldtrips to the library, bookstore, computer center, or other campus location. Students often comment, with surprise, on how quickly the day passes. The secret is to keep a sense that everything is in constant motion! In part, I accomplish this by including more things than I think I can accomplish in any eight-hour period. (I always prioritize the segments so some may be expendable, but we also cover more than I had anticipated.) The purpose is to maintain a high level of engagement and to increase endurance among the students throughout the entire compressed schedule.

Advance Assignment

The compressed schedule gives our class the opportunity to examine one of the cornerstones of Knowles's (1984) foundational work on the adult learner—the idea of the self-directed learner. I use an advance assignment to begin talking about this concept, although I reinforce it with many other applications throughout the course. For instance, later during classes on Saturday or Sunday, we discuss the characteristics of the adult learner so that students can see how their experience with the advance assignment relates to their own experience with self-directed learning.

As an advance assignment, students are asked to read a portion of the textbook, covering any material we will examine during the first night. This, however, isn't a very meaningful portion of the assignment (although the students often initially think of it as the primary expectation). There are three aspects of this initial assignment that begin to tap into the adult learner's skill sets. Before the night is over, students will have displayed their writing, speaking, and listening skills, though they are not initially articulated to the student in that way. In fact, by working in a learner-centered classroom, the students may not even realize that these activities are taking place, since they are seldom the focus of the activities they encounter.

Course Content

Students who have taken this course always remark about the food we provide with the course! We begin the first night with pizza (it is indicated in the advance assignment). As the new students enter, the pizza has already been delivered, the tables are set up in a large circle (I'm sitting at one of them), and there is a packet for each student so they understand that they are expected to join the circle. As they enter, I welcome them, ask them to tape up one of their advance assignments for their classmates to see (more about that later), and invite them to get some food and drink before joining the circle. There is something very powerful about sharing a meal, especially with strangers with whom you're about to spend the next three days.

To begin class, our first experience involves a dual task. The students are asked to briefly relate the journey that brought them to this classroom. At the same time, the remaining students are required to take good notes (using listening and note-taking skills) in order to "become" one of their classmates for a second time around. Since they don't know who they will present themselves as, they listen attentively. When it is their turn to share what they initially heard, it becomes very clear if they are having trouble taking notes. We later talk about how to address this problem.

I also emphasize the importance of learning everyone's name. For the remainder of the course, students are encouraged to use their classmates' names whenever they interact. Most of them know everybody's name by the end of the first night.

There are a number of issues that relate to the student's "journey" story. First of all, evidence suggests that people are more phobic about speaking in public than any other activity. While the stories are supposed to be brief, it is usually easier for students to tell their own story than any other class recitation. At the same time, these stories often prove incredibly powerful. Half the class has been in tears by the end of this session simply because they were so moved by what they heard. But there is another purpose for these stories as well and somebody usually remarks about this before the weekend is over. The stories help the students understand that they are not alone and that many others share the same sorts of challenges, sacrifices, obstacles, motivations, and dreams. This revelation is often the beginning of their transformation.

The remainder of the evening is crammed full of an array of activities and learning opportunities. These start with a careful review of the course syllabus. But once again, it is not for the sole purpose of reviewing the syllabus that we enter into this event. It is a perfect opportunity to discuss *what* a syllabus is, *how* it is supposed to work, its *contractual* nature, and the *expectations* associated with it. In this way, learning is taking place at two levels. My syllabus is rather extensive. Since I can't possibly capture every detail of our time in class for this chapter, I have included the course syllabus in Appendix 7A at the end of this chapter. There are, however, a few of the course elements I can address at this time.

Food

Because I want to make the most of our time together, I structure class lunches for Saturday and Sunday. On Saturday, I bring them to the school's main dining room. Typically, this is the area where "traditional" students eat. Even though there are no overt threats from these students, it can be intimidating for any adult learner to enter this environment. Adult students frequently say that they don't feel like they belong there. The intention of the dining room visit is to reinforce the notion that the facility is available to anyone in the college community, and these new adult learners are now part of that community. Likewise, on Sunday, we use the more formal dining room on campus for brunch. In this case, the school's chapter of Alpha Sigma Lambda (ASL) serves as host. At least one ASL member sits at each table with the students. During the meal, conversations tend to revolve around the hosts' previous classroom experiences based on their veteran status. At the end of the meal, one of the ASL members speaks briefly about the benefits and criteria for membership. (Membership in this group has significantly increased since we began using this format.) One additional benefit of this kind of experience is that it helps the students become acclimated to various buildings on campus as they walk to and from the meals.

Near the end of the final day, the class begins to "decompress" so that students can adjust to their pretransformation lives. I devote extensive time to the topic of the final project. Having already supplied models of successful examples, I now talk about strategies and more explicit expectations. Since we have already spoken during the final day about time management and the need for organization, the final project concerns are a natural extension. This discussion reminds the students that their grade will be contingent on this project, so I make certain that all questions and concerns are addressed before moving on to our concluding topics.

For closure, students lead a discussion about the bumper stickers they created as part of their advance assignment. Since the bumper stickers have been on display during the entire class, students have had ample time to examine them. As each student presents his or her bumper sticker and explains the message contained in the text and images, it is natural to reflect on the difference between these presentations and the initial commentary just two short days previously. It is immediately evident why the course is described as a transformation.

Then the class completes a series of evaluations. The students each write a line or two, along with their signature, in the course guest book so that their participation and comments are documented, and others can read the entries of the groups that preceded them. And suddenly (almost too quickly for some, judging by how students are likely to remain around after this final meeting), the course meetings are over, with only the final project still outstanding.

Final Project

One of the important activities associated with this course is reflection or introspection. During the two weeks after the completion of the course, students are expected to tap heavily into their learning experiences and life history. For my class, the final project comprises a number of interrelated papers that draw upon the students' writing, organizational, and introspection skills. The following components are included:

- A reflective journal that documents the student's time from the first class through the two weeks that follow the course meetings

- An educational autobiography in which the student describes the formal and informal learning that has taken place throughout his or her life (this often leads to students pursuing prior learning assessment credits once they realize how extensive their learning experiences have been)

- A personal mission statement which provides the student with a foundation or solid frame of reference as further studies are pursued

- A degree completion plan that enables the student to identify crucial courses and a workable timeline for planning ahead

Lessons Learned

- *This type of course contributes to good retention.* Because of the bonding, the skill development, and the survivor strategies, students who complete this course express a greater level of confidence and commitment to perseverance. This might be attributable to the high correlation between perseverance and achievement.

- *High standards and expectations for a course like this create a legitimate foundation for further student development.* Many students who completed this course note that they were surprised by its difficulty. But they also note that the course served as a wakeup for what college-level work entails.

- *This course provides meaningful services to adult learners by demystifying the college experience.* One of the main objectives of this course is to acquaint adult learners with how things "work" on the campus by covering everything from the differences between assistant, associate, and full professor to which courses are likely to fill faster than others. By making myself a resource and being willing to respond to students' curiosity about the campus and collegiate life, I find that adult learners in this course are more likely to be aware of many of the nuances that their peers are apt to miss.

- *If you define your program as "learner-centered" or "adult-friendly," this course reinforces your message.* Incoming students who seek a support system or elevated sense of caring from an institution will probably feel that this course delivers on that expectation.

- *Be careful not to overload the enrollment for this course.* Each instructor may differ slightly in this regard, but I have found that when I allow more than 20 students to enroll, it detracts from the overall impact of the class. I attribute this to how much I am limited in providing personalized attention for each student. Furthermore, the group dynamics, which are critical for a course like this, change dramatically when there are more than 20 students in the course.

- *Always plan on more topics than you believe you can cover during the class.* While one group of students may want to talk about stress management (for instance) for a very long time, the next might not want to spend any time discussing it. Adults don't like to have their time wasted, so I try to have an array of topics we can cover.

- *Recognize that you're always being scrutinized. It's good to keep to a schedule, but demonstrating flexibility is also desirable.* Since I want the students to be as flexible as possible in their own approach to their education, I find that modeling often tends to have a disproportionate impact on them. For instance, one time when the class was supposed to use a computer lab, a graduate student wouldn't let us enter. I remained patient even though he was somewhat abrasive, and we finally agreed that the class would return in one hour. Almost every student wrote in their journals about how impressed they were with my demeanor, although at the time I didn't think anyone even noticed.

References

Ashar, H., & Skenes, R. (1993, Winter). Can Tinto's student departure model be applied to nontraditional students? *Adult Education Quarterly, 43*(2), 90–100.

Bash, L., Lighty, K., & Tebrock, D. (1999). Utilizing a "transformation course" to assist returning adult learners. *Proceedings of Adult Higher Education Alliance, 19,* 1–5. Retrieved September 21, 2004, from http://www.ahea.org/Utilizing_a_transformation_course.htm

Brookfield, S. D. (1986). *Understanding and facilitating adult learning.* San Francisco, CA: Jossey-Bass.

Chaffee, E. E. (1998). Listening to the people we serve. In W. G. Tierney (Ed.), *The responsive university: Restructuring for high performance* (pp. 13–37). Baltimore, MD: Johns Hopkins University Press.

Kerka, S. (1995) *Adult learner retention revisited* (ERIC Digest No. 166.) Columbus, OH: ERIC Clearinghouse on Adult, Career, and Vocational Education. Retrieved September 21, 2004, from http://www.ericdigests.org/1996-3/adult.htm

Knowles, M. S. (1984). *Andragogy in action: Applying modern principles of adult learning.* San Francisco, CA: Jossey-Bass.

Morrell, A., & O'Connor, M. A. (2002). Introduction. In E. O'Sullivan, A. Morrell, & M. A. O'Connor (Eds.), *Expanding the boundaries of transformative learning* (pp. xv–xx). New York, NY: Palgrave.

Schlossberg, N. K., Lynch, A. Q., & Chickering, A. W. (1989). *Improving higher education environments for adults.* San Francisco, CA: Jossey-Bass.

U.S. Department of Education, National Center for Education Statistics. (2002). *The condition of education 2002* (NCES 2002–025). Washington, DC: U.S. Government Printing Office. Retrieved September 21, 2004, from http://www.inpathways.net/high%20school%20academic%20preparation.pdf

Appendix 7A
Syllabus
COL (162)
Principles of Adult Learning

Class: Friday, January 9, 6:00 p.m.–9:00 p.m.

            Saturday & Sunday, January 10 & 11, 9:00 a.m.–5:00 p.m.

Textbook: *New Beginnings: A Guide for Adult Learners and Returning Students* (2nd Edition) Prentice Hall (ISBN 0-13-060738-X)

Instructor: Dr. Lee Bash

            Bonds Hall, 106

Course Description

This *two credit-hour seminar,* based on a *letter grade,* is the foundation for adults enrolled in the Evening & Weekend College at Baldwin-Wallace (B-W). It may be used toward degree completion as a *free elective* and is designed to help new and returning students make the transition to the academic world. This seminar stresses *critical reading, active discussion, and reflective writing.* Readings are drawn from the fields of education, philosophy, literature, psychology, and the social and natural sciences. We will use the classroom and outside assignments as a *forum* to explore student's philosophies of *education, learning styles, understanding of the liberal arts,* and ways of relating experiences to academic pursuits. It is this course that serves as the gateway to the adult student's journey as a lifelong learner.

Objectives and Outcomes

The objectives of this seminar are:

- To give adults a sense of themselves as learners
- To develop a sense of the academic community, its rigors, and its pleasures—especially at B-W
- To enable students to acquire the skills requisite for academic life

- To assist students with tools and strategies in dealing with the personal components associated with the pursuit of adult learning

- To enable students to understand the full potential of a liberal arts education

- To introduce and orient the new adult student to B-W

- To familiarize students with the opportunities and experiences they are likely to encounter in pursuit of their degree

- To assess the student's current level of skill development and capacity

- To assist the student with setting long-term educational goals

- To enable students to develop good relationships with their instructors

- To help the student feel comfortable and productive in class

The Outcomes for This Seminar

Through in-class presentations, papers, and the use of a reflective journal, the student will be able to:

- Identify personally relevant goals and propose reasonable means for achieving them

- Recognize and describe the learning value of his or her past and present experiences

- Develop a philosophy of education that corresponds to his or her own values and assumptions

Instructional Methods to Achieve These Goals

The following activities are utilized to accomplish the above-stated objectives and outcomes:

- Selections from texts and articles that will introduce, integrate, and direct the class discussions and give examples of the interrelatedness of the liberal arts at B-W

- The use of various assessment and evaluation instruments designed for placement and assisting the student's growth and development

- A reflective journal on the text and experiences to enable the student to discuss reactions, concerns, observations, and questions

- Demonstrations using B-W facilities and systems

- Discussions, debates, reports, presentations, and the use of media

- Activities designed to promote strong foundations and positive experiences for adult students at B-W

Attendance Policy

Since the material contained in this course is explicitly designed for the new adult learner at Baldwin-Wallace College and often cannot be obtained through any other source, students are expected to attend all classes and to be on time for classes in which they are registered. Because this course is an immersion, attendance for all classes is mandatory.

Course Requirements

1) Attendance and participation in class are essential requirements for this course. It is expected that participants meet all timelines regarding assignments. *All students should be prepared to contribute thoughts and insights to the discussions of readings and other material presented.* The quality of participation by all class members is critical to a productive and meaningful experience in this course. Because of this, a portion of each participant's overall grade will be based on participation, further defined as contributing during in-class discussions and learning tasks, and/or communicating thoughts and insights through your journal entries.

2) Homework assignments at the conclusion of the first two classes must be completed and done at a satisfactory level. Participants are expected to complete all readings listed in the course outline prior to the respective class session.

3) At the conclusion of the course, an *analytical/reflective journal* (see handout, "*Reflectere—To Bend Back*" for details) containing entries on assigned readings and class experiences, featuring an analysis of the main ideas in the text and a personal reflection on it must be submitted in a final form. It will be graded based upon thoroughness

and comprehensive coverage of the material presented in class. As a safeguard to the student, no part of the grade will be based upon *opinions* expressed by the student although these will be encouraged in the expectation that future courses can be improved. It will, however, be graded upon the thoroughness and completeness of your work as well as your organizational and writing skills. As in all assignments, the final version should be typed. The following questions should minimally be addressed in the journal:

- Develop your own mission statement and philosophy of education as it corresponds to the values and assumptions espoused in your mission statement.

- What have you learned about yourself from the self-assessment inventories and how will that knowledge change your approach to study and class work?

- What's the most challenging aspect of being an adult student?

- List the career goals you have right now. How will your college program help you to achieve those goals?

- Address your writing skills. How do you assess your writing abilities? What areas concern you? What have previous instructors said about your writing? What has been your most satisfying writing experience? What has been your least satisfying writing experience? Identify five goals you have as a writer.

- Your overall assessment and reaction to this course should be included as well. Since your feedback regarding the instructor will have already been obtained, you may restrict your observations to the strong points of the class and/or recommendations on how to improve future presentations of the course.

- The journal should contain your reflections between the first evening of class and the remainder of the two weeks—at least up through the following Thursday evening.

4) An *Educational Autobiography.* This paper will reflect your experiences with formal education beginning as early as you can recall up to the present date. It should be written in first person and include factual information and commentary that reflects past and present

feelings about your experiences, significant events, and how you were impacted by these experiences. There is no page requirement or limit.

5) A *Degree Plan*. How long will it take you to complete your studies? (Determine how many credit hours per semester or year; identify which courses you are required to complete that are infrequently offered, etc.)

6) Your reflective journal, Educational Autobiography, and Degree Plan materials are all to be turned in to the Office of Lifelong Learning no later than noon on Saturday, January 24th. If you submit your materials electronically or at the receptionist's desk in Bonds 102 (Evening & Weekend College), you may then retrieve them after Saturday, February 7th.

7) Projects handed in late will reflect a significant reduction in the final grade.

Criteria in Grading

Grading is based on the quality and depth of your work in the following areas:

Attendance and class participation	25%
Reflective journal, educational autobiography, & degree plan entries	40%
Reading assignments & homework	35%

Personal Disabilities

Any student with a documented disability (e.g., physical, learning, psychological, vision, hearing, etc.) who needs to arrange accommodations must contact both the instructor and Disability Services at the beginning of each term.

Class schedule

Friday, 6:00 p.m.–9:00 p.m.

- Get acquainted pizza dinner

- Welcome and orientation

- Testimonial

- Your syllabus, your contract

- How to develop a journal (handout)

- Learning styles

- Scavenger hunt (fact-finding mission by team)

- Scavenger report

- Pre-assignments: why they're important & "hand yours in now"

- Levels of learning

- Saturday lunch details

- Overnight assignment (Read Chapters 5 & 8 in the book, "Lessons from Adult Learning," "Guidelines for Success," & "A Question of Degrees")

Saturday, 9:00 a.m.–5:00 p.m.
(note: we will start promptly—the sooner we start, the sooner we finish)

- Review of previous class

- Preview of the day/overnight assignments

- The adult learner

- College-level writing: expectations and strategies

- Advising strategies—the two year plan (fall schedule)

- Your catalog, your contract

- Financial aid for adult learners (10:00) Jason Florack

- Tour of the library

- Group lunch (we will all eat together)

- New student IDs—ID office

- Study groups—special opportunities for the adult learner

- How to become an "A" student

- Test-taking strategies

- Obtaining credit from CLEP, College Credit Recommendation Service, or proficiency examinations

- Obtaining credit from Prior Learning Assessment (PLA)–COL 163

- Overnight assignment (Read "Learning in the 21st Century," "The Future of Colleges–9 Inevitable Changes," & Chapters 4 & 7 in the book)

Sunday, 9:00 a.m.–5:00 p.m.

- Review of previous class

- Preview of the day/overnight assignments

- Your new email account

- The RegExpress

- Writing assessment

- Strategies for research

- Plagiarism

- What does "liberal arts education" mean for me?

- Group lunch—Colony Room (we will all eat together)

- Educational goals—strategies and opportunities

- Your degree plan

- The Ladder of Inference

- Stress management for the adult learner (pp. 48–52)

- Listening and note-taking

- Writing a clear mission statement (first draft)

- Time management

- Educational autobiography

- Preparing final projects and term papers

- Final overview, questions, and closure

- IDEA teacher assessment

How to Obtain an "A" in This Course

As you will learn in this class, students typically decide what their final grade will be based on how hard they are willing to work to achieve what they consider acceptable. An "A" grade implies *superlative* work in all aspects. *Students who are inattentive, don't fully and actively participate in discussion, aren't thoroughly organized in the way they present their thinking, and/or don't display the highest standards of editing and writing can't expect to receive an A.*

Furthermore, since reflection and introspection are so important to the outcomes in this course, the successful student needs to make a commitment to the meaningful pursuit of these objectives so that he or she can articulate the insights and values obtained from these activities. Simply going through the process on a more casual level does not satisfy A-level work.

Finally, like almost every course, "A" work should be considered as extraordinary. If you desire an A, your task is to determine how you will make your work—your product—*more outstanding than everyone else's.* If you are not very intentional about these strategies, the chances are you will *not* receive an A in this or any other course.

Part III

Faculty Development: A Key to Instructional Effectiveness

8

Adjunct Faculty Training

Stuart Noble-Goodman, W. Hubbard Segur

There are numerous models and rubrics in place for the recruitment, training, and development of adjunct faculty, and for assessing the effectiveness of those systems. This chapter will outline the development and implementation of the system in place at the University of Redlands School of Business (URSB). While Redlands might not be typical in terms of its very sizable adjunct faculty pool, the model is readily scalable; indeed, the resources required to implement this sort of system might be considerably less at a school with fewer adjuncts, sections, or programs.

The program described here engages adjunct faculty members at all stages of their career with the institution, from hiring through professional renewal. While this chapter is nominally about adjunct faculty development, we have included descriptions of the hiring and mentoring processes because we feel these processes are inseparable from a holistic approach to adjunct faculty development.

In addition, it should be noted that while we refer consistently to the adjunct faculty as the focus of this development program, the full-time tenure-track faculty fully participate and derive substantial benefits from this program as well. Finally, we have included some data that we have collected regarding our new, expanded development program. We include this data less as an authoritative analysis of our success (since we have only evaluated the program for two years, offering limited longitudinal information) than as an example of the assessment of efforts that should be integral to any formal system of development.

In this chapter, we will briefly discuss the evolution of faculty development activities at a business school housed in a relatively small liberal arts university with a substantial, geographically distributed adult student enrollment and large adjunct contingent. We will discuss the lessons learned during that development, and review data on best practices emergent from a holistic adjunct faculty training program in that context.

Today's academy has a larger reliance on part-time faculty than ever before. As a result, higher education has begun to struggle with issues surrounding the equitable and effective integration of adjunct faculty into the fuller fabric of the university. Institutions with significant adult student populations are especially likely to rely on higher numbers of adjunct faculty, particularly with programs that utilize geographically scattered learning sites. Thus the pressure to construct a meaningful and productive relationship with adjunct faculty should be considered as acute for these institutions, since they probably rely on these very adjuncts to deliver a consistently excellent educational experience to large numbers of their adult learners.

Everyone benefits when adjunct faculty are integrated into curricular planning so they too can deliver educational goals set in individual courses and at the program level. As accreditation agencies increase emphasis on the ability of schools to demonstrate learning outcomes, adjunct faculty development takes on even more significance. In addition, professional development programs can serve as powerful incentives to increase adjunct faculty commitment to an institution. If comprehensive enough, such programs can also serve several other purposes: They can engage adjuncts deeply as institutional stakeholders, function as a key component of their evaluation portfolio, and ensure that a high level of pedagogical and substantive consistency are present in an institution's classrooms—especially in distributed learning contexts, where such consistency can be more difficult to achieve.

Institutional Context

Established in southern California in 1976, the University of Redlands Whitehead College combined numerous professional programs under one umbrella, with an emphasis on business, education, and liberal studies. Eventually, the size and scope of the adult programs led the university to establish separate schools of education and business, in 2000 and 2001, respectively. The mission of both professional schools is to provide a liberal arts education to working adults from diverse locations who have a wide range of abilities. The School of Education also offers undergraduate degrees to the university's traditional day students.

Over time, the adult programs had built a strong adjunct faculty screening and training process. With the separation of the schools, however, this process had begun to drift. Without consistent renewal and refreshment, it became less effective, as most of the academic programs in the School had been revised in the preceding two years or were in the process of revision.

There was another broader issue connected to the program revisions. A number of substantial changes in the school had affected the adjunct faculty. We had modified the way we scheduled their teaching assignments, changed the administrative structure of the regions where they taught, produced a new handbook (with their assistance), and modified numerous administrative processes that affected them. Consequently, they became confused about some of these administrative issues and developments, so we felt it was critical to gather them together and communicate the nature and rationale of these changes directly to them.

In response to these concerns, in the fall of 2001 the dean of the URSB asked the faculty and senior academic staff to create a comprehensive plan for adjunct faculty renewal. She appointed a working group of faculty, staff, and administrators to undertake this effort. The guiding principle for this process was that it was collaborative, inclusive, and faculty driven. Otherwise, the problems associated with stakeholder disenfranchisement would inevitably apply.

In Redlands' case, the dean appointed a senior faculty member with experience in faculty development to lead the development team in collaboration with the associate dean. It is psychologically important for the adjunct faculty to see support for their development at the highest levels, and if possible, to be personally engaged in the construction of the program.

We articulated the intended outcomes of the program and then identified any significant constraints. Together, these factors informed the implementation plan and determined what needed to be done to meet the intended outcomes, helping us to understand our limitations and parameters.

Setting Goals and Creating the Initial Design

Setting Goals

It is important at this first stage to establish a collective vision of faculty professional development in the unit—including the adjunct faculty. A number of important questions arise: Does the mission support faculty development? What is the senior administration's commitment to professional development? What are the faculty's (and administration's) expectations regarding the outcomes of such activity? What type of institution and what kind of academic unit is conducting the training?

On a more mundane level: How does the infrastructure interact with this project? How large a population is the development program going to serve? Is that population geographically dispersed? If it is, is the program "going" to the adjuncts, or will the adjuncts be asked to come to a central location? How diverse are the programs or degrees in which the faculty teach? Will faculty development be considered part of the service obligation of the adjuncts, or is this training elective?

In Redlands' case, both the senior administration and the dean ardently supported faculty development. The unit's mission included a commitment to producing quality professionals, and that included the adjunct faculty. The faculty hoped that the program would increase the educational effectiveness of the adjuncts, support and streamline their communication with the adjuncts, and enhance the adjunct's professional and pedagogical understanding of the various academic programs and their intended learning outcomes.

It was the dean's hope that the development program would augment the professional academic qualifications of the adjuncts in light of the rigorous standards expressed by the professional school accreditation body. Coincidentally, the regional accreditation body, the Western Association of Schools and Colleges, was also moving toward "assurance of learning" standards, so the unit goals and institutional goals converged.

Because of the revision of several programs, we felt it important to bring our adjuncts (as well as our full-time faculty from diverse programs) up to date on the larger programmatic academic picture. The school had received feedback from students and adjuncts that the adjuncts were teaching in academic silos. One goal was to establish a cumulative knowledge base that would allow adjunct faculty to broaden their perspective beyond the courses they taught. Because of the information and communication gaps inherent in these silos, it was not always clear to the adjuncts what the continuity was from one course to another, how the skill sets built upon one another sequentially, or what the overall learning outcomes were for each program.

Creating the Initial Design

We needed to design ways to integrate our new faculty recruits into this process, and we needed to incorporate a mentoring/assessment piece into the overall plan. During the spring of 2002 the dean of the URSB proposed a sequence of semiannual faculty development conferences (locally referred to as training) with a dual purpose of increasing teaching effectiveness among both full-time and part-time faculty and initiating an institutional commitment to dedicated adjunct faculty to enhance their professional academic qualifications.

The initial plan was to hold these full-day conferences on successive Saturdays in August and March. A team of faculty, administrators, staff, and regional directors shared in building the agenda. Faculty members involved in the planning focused on designing teaching effectiveness workshops. Program directors focused on comprehensive program goals and curricular coherence across courses. Regional directors sought to clarify administrative matters and to build regional community.

The faculty designers proposed eight workshops centered on the classroom. The objectives for the proposal stated:

> These sessions provide a unified, coherent foundation of teaching effectiveness at URSB. Our intent is that the sessions will build over time, encouraging incremental improvement of instructional performance . . . and allow the faculty to develop common language and competencies in areas crucial for educational effectiveness. . . . The classroom evaluation of instructors will be at least partly based upon the performance indicators established in the training.

Each of the workshops was designed to touch on universal issues related to working with adult students in an accelerated format. Topics included Accelerated Course Design and Delivery, Indicators of Teaching Excellence, Case Study Methodology, Enhancing Academic Honesty, Focus on Critical Thinking, and Assessment of Student Learning. Each session was designed to be a facilitated exchange of ideas, yet promised the delivery of at least three learning objectives that were linked to the classroom. We had long since acknowledged that the keys to successful adjunct workshops were open discussions and lessons learned that could be integrated immediately into the classroom.

Constraints

One of the central constraints on a faculty development program is financial. Your budget will have a significant impact on your decisions. Put simply, what can you afford to do? How will you deploy limited resources to maximum effect? In terms of assessment, how will you demonstrate to institutional stakeholders (deans, senior administrators, trustees) that your development program is effective and warrants continued investment?

In our case, we were dealing with roughly 200 adjuncts. They were dispersed across about 10,000 square miles of southern California. Another major constraint was time. Since most of our adjuncts are working professionals, holding sessions during the workweek was not feasible, so our program had to take place on the weekend. With so much information to communicate, the duration of the session became an issue. How much time was reasonable? How could we involve the adjuncts in a process that might be occurring at some distance from them and maximize the experience?

Some other constraint issues to consider might include: What facilities are available on your campus? Is there adequate space to host an event the size you're contemplating? What technology is required? Are there resource people available to support your program? If not, do you have the resources to secure the support personnel and/or hardware that will be required? Are you going to establish a reward structure—mileage, honoraria, professional development credit?

The method we chose to connect with the adjuncts was to establish a broad theme—The Redlands Way—that was ambiguous enough to include various thematic strands under a single rubric, but would allow the adjunct participants to help define the substance of the theme. Ultimately, The Redlands Way—what it means to teach at Redlands, and how that meaning is implemented in the classroom—would be defined in collaboration with the adjuncts.

Establishing such a theme would also allow us to construct a model of potential activities—workshops, large and small group sessions, breakouts, and formal presentations—that would give us the flexibility to communicate a variety of information under a single umbrella. This theme had the additional benefits of piquing their interest (what is The Redlands Way?), and providing a flexible, capacious framework under which we could communally work without thematic constraint.

Outcomes Assessment

Having established the mission of the development program, the next step is to identify outcomes that can be measured at the end of training. Redlands established several outcomes, some of which were more readily measurable than others. Faculty satisfaction, for instance, could be surveyed with ease at the midpoints and conclusion of sessions, but whether the training would have a positive impact in the classroom was a more complex outcome that included many factors.

Once the measurable outcomes were established, the assessment instruments were designed. In Redlands' case, the instruments were surveys of participants, student satisfaction surveys in the classroom, administrative and peer classroom observations, and retention figures. Each of these dimensions would yield trends over time that could be combined into a relatively accurate performance profile. This, in turn, could be used for future strategic planning of development activities.

Implementation

Having established the broad goals and design of the adjunct development program, and identified our constraints and outcomes, we began to flesh out the details of the program. A critical factor in the successful planning process is to involve staff and administrative personnel throughout. Faculty probably do not want to hear this, but staff's ability to execute the plan smoothly is critical to success. Involving staff in high-level planning sessions from the outset has three primary benefits: 1) staff are able to identify important potential stumbling blocks that faculty and administrators often overlook, 2) their inclusion provides a framework in which staff are able to improvise when necessary and remain consistent with goals and processes, and 3) staff input at this level assures a stakeholder mentality and commitment to success for all concerned.

Collectively, we identified several areas of need:

- Pedagogical training to enhance educational effectiveness in the class-room, linked to The Redlands Way— including the mission statement

- Programmatic informational sessions, at which adjuncts would receive program "roadmaps"

- Summaries of best practices for sharing among the entire faculty

- Regional information sessions covering administrative issues and consistency of policy implementation

- Mentoring and support sessions for new, probationary faculty

- High-profile keynote speakers as a featured attraction

- Topical sessions on issues such as grading, rigor, and academic integrity

- Instructional tools such as Blackboard

- Mission driven goals such as ethics and writing across the curriculum training

Because of the range of stakeholder interests and concerns that reflected so many important and substantial areas of need, the planners determined that two full days on successive Saturdays would be required—once in the fall, and once again in the spring. This allowed us to divide a large group of faculty in half while reducing the number of programs that needed to be addressed in the roadmap sessions. Mentoring sessions and the regional information sessions would occur in both fall and spring, while The Redlands Way would provide a unifying thread across programs, regions, and time. The keynote speaker was deferred until the spring (our inaugural workshops were in the fall), as were the topical sessions. The best practices piece was included in the fall.

Making these decisions at the outset allowed the staff to begin detailed preparation for the implementation phase. For example, with a large body of professional practitioners who consult, work full-time, and travel extensively serving as adjuncts, it was important that invitations were issued several months before the event. And because there were space issues on campus, booking the best space possible required substantial advance time.

Staff Issues

The staff extracted a number of points for success as they coordinated several sessions.

- If possible, hire, select, or appoint a coordinator who is experienced in event/conference planning involving substantial groups of people.

- Adopt a theme or image (e.g., The Redlands Way) for the event and use the theme for every event.

- Use the date of the event as the baseline for planning. Back everything up from that date. For example, if your event is March 20, you should consider the following timeline:

    - Coordinator establishes timeline for event

    - Room booked 6–12 months in advance

    - Initial meeting of planning committee nine months in advance

    - Final list of invitees three months in advance

    - Final invitation list/invite letter two and one-half months in advance

    - Invitations in mail two months in advance

    - RSVP deadline two weeks in advance

- Develop and use a pre-event planning checklist. Review regularly and always confirm deliverables and expectations with staff.

- Develop and use a mockup of the agenda at all coordination meetings.

- Develop the binders/handouts you'll be using as early as possible, and refine them as the event approaches. This "keepsake" is a very important tool in terms of the training and the perception of the attendees on the level of professionalism involved.

- Establish vendors—especially printers—well in advance. There may be opportunities to obtain discounted or free materials or services, and these should be pursued. Emphasize the importance of deadlines, and always allow for several days overrun.

- At least 30 days before the event, put yourself in the shoes of the participants and literally walk through the entire day—from invitation to departure—and make adjustments accordingly.

- Two days before the event, walk through it verbally with the support staff, making sure that everyone knows and understands their role. Emphasize that there will be problems, and have everyone anticipate how these can be handled efficiently and successfully.

Individual Activities

What follows is a breakdown of the different activities that comprise our training, including a detailed example of how one of the plenary sessions was delivered.

Mentoring

Many aspects of adult education are often different from what a faculty member is likely to encounter with traditional students. Courses regularly occur on nights and weekends, often in an accelerated format. When working adults come to an evening course after a full day's work, they're often tired and stressed out, and they're facing class sessions that run from two to four hours. Without substantial support and training, adjunct faculty may lack strategies to maximize the learning that occurs in their classrooms. It is in this context that a robust faculty mentoring program can pay substantial dividends.

At Redlands, new adjuncts are assigned a mentor after successfully completing the initial assessment process. During that process, the courses for which the adjunct is qualified to teach are identified. In consultation with the various program directors, a single initial course is identified, and a master teacher of that course—either an experienced adjunct or a full-time faculty member—is assigned. The adjunct attends each session of the mentor's course. At some point, usually the second or third course of six, the probationary adjunct will team-teach a session with the mentor. The adjunct will then teach an entire session by himself or herself. Both of these sessions are observed and evaluated by the mentor as well as the students. If the performance is satisfactory, the adjunct will be assigned a section of that course during the next term. The mentor and probationary adjunct continue to meet, and in the next term, the mentor will observe at least two additional sessions taught by the candidate. In addition, the academic officer with responsibility for the adjunct will observe and evaluate at least two sessions taught by the candidate, and the program director will also observe and assess. In this way the institution is provided with multiple data points and perspectives on the candidate's performance, resulting in a high level of confidence that the candidate will be successful in the classroom. One of the most significant benefits of this system is the immediate feedback that observers provide the candidate.

Program Roadmaps

These sessions are designed to familiarize faculty with the overall structure of a program. More particularly, they provide all faculty—both adjuncts and full-time—with a clear sense of program and course-level (individual syllabi) learning outcomes. The goal of these sessions is to locate the faculty on a curricular continuum so they understand why the curricula are designed in a specific sequence and how the courses build upon each other. This is critical in all institutional models, but especially important in those that employ large numbers of adjuncts. With a large cadre of adjuncts, it is easy for adjuncts to see themselves as "an economics instructor" or "a statistics instructor" without having a clear sense of why their course is placed where it is, why the previous and subsequent courses are ordered in a certain way, and how their course is substantively and educationally linked to other courses. Such confusion can seriously undermine the academic integrity of courses and programs, as individual faculty are unclear on what skills and knowledge students should bring to their course, and what core skills and knowledge students must take from their course to be successful in subsequent courses. Such confusion can lead to a disjointed educational experience, in which students are left with a knowledge deficit in certain courses, and possibly a knowledge surfeit (vis-à-vis core skills and knowledge) in other courses. Student frustration with such intellectual dislocation can ultimately lead to reduced student satisfaction and higher attrition rates. In addition, both regional and professional accrediting bodies have increased emphasis on learning assurance. Without a definitive understanding of the outcomes toward which they're teaching, it is difficult for adjuncts to support a learning assurance effort. Given that institutions are devoting considerable financial, administrative, and faculty resources to this effort, it is easy to understand the importance of development in this area.

In Redlands' case, program directors were asked to create substantial workshops of two or more hours that began by explaining the global learning outcomes for their programs, and why those outcomes had been established. Such sessions included the role of introductory courses, the rationale for course sequencing, and the manner in which cumulative knowledge bases and skill sets are incorporated into capstone experiences. Program directors then elucidated individual course learning objectives and how individual assignments supported those objectives. Finally, course inclusion or exclusion decisions were explained. An example from the MBA program road map is illustrative.

In redesigning the MBA program, Redlands' faculty decided to include a course on the history of political economy. The course included readings from Marx, Keynes, Locke, and Friedman. While this initially struck many of the adjuncts as an odd choice—given the rare appearance of such courses in standard MBA programs—the course directly supported the liberal arts mission of the university, and expressed the faculty's desire to ground MBA students in the foundational texts of capitalism and critiques of that economic system. Without being exposed to what the course was intended to achieve, adjuncts would not have been able to capitalize on the expanded educational opportunities that the course gave them. For example, it enabled them to begin a conversation on the various critiques of globalization in courses as divergent as economics, finance, and international business. Communicating this aspect of the curriculum answered questions the adjuncts might have had about the efficacy of such a course, and allowed them to brainstorm with other colleagues in real time about the instructional possibilities this course might provide them in their own classrooms.

Best Practices

Professional practitioner adjunct faculty, in particular, respond well to best practice sessions. Just as adult students are eager to gain practical knowledge they can take to their workplace, their faculty are eager to utilize a toolset of pedagogical strategies that will allow them to be successful in the classroom. With the longer sessions associated with the accelerated format common to adult programs, faculty need an array of teaching strategies to engage a student population that needs to maximize every limited minute.

Here is an example of one of the best practices workshops that was part of a plenary session titled "Indicators of Teaching Excellence."

This workshop was presented on the fourth conference gathering. The faculty design proposal subtitled it "URSB's Best Practices" and commented: "Instructor behaviors, techniques and strategies that have proven to enhance teaching quality at URSB are presented. . . . Classroom instructor evaluation is often linked to successful implementation of (such) practices." At the conclusion of each workshop, participants will be prepared to: (a) Implement new strategies and revise current practices (where appropriate); (b) Assess the benefits and/or shortcomings of those practices; and (c) Access a colleague network to discuss classroom techniques.

This fourth edition of our conference attracted 116 adjuncts, our largest gathering to date. After a brief introduction, we broke into groups of 25–30 with each group assigned to a side room off the auditorium. On the walls of each side room were some twenty Post-it Easel Sheets spaced evenly around the room at eye level. Each sheet had a heading related to some aspect of teaching or a classroom situation. The headings were designed to encourage candid responses. They included: "What 'low-stakes' student work is most successful?" "How do you accommodate differences in student preparation?" "Your agenda for tonight's session is completed and it is 9:20 pm. Now what?" (our classes run to 10 pm). "Complete: 'I am most challenged in the classroom when . . .'." "Late student papers—how do you respond?" "How do you organize break-out groups?" "What is the maximum time for an effective lecture?" "Grade points for effort and/or improvement—appropriate?"

On entering the room, participants were handed a broad-point marker and told to circulate and write. Participants moved about the room, reading their colleagues' comments and adding their own. Two formats for creating discussion on the posted questions emerged. One had the entire group in open session, probing authors on particularly interesting or novel comments on the more challenging topics. A second approach was to divide into subgroups of five or six with each subgroup marking up the most insightful comment for each poster. The most frequent comment from participants at the conclusion of the exercise was on how helpful it was to read how others responded to the situations posted.

The posters from all four sections of this exercise were transcribed with the responses for each topic collected and summarized. They were then electronically posted for faculty review and additional comment. Four of the topics brought forth such an interesting diversity of responses that they were earmarked for further discussion at a future conference gathering. Faculty participants gave this workshop the highest rating of all the conferences' plenary exercises.

Keynote Speakers

In deciding whether to use a high-profile external speaker, it is worth weighing the relative merits of this investment. One substantial value a keynote speaker brings is excitement and anticipation about the event, and possibly even media coverage. High-profile speakers carry a great deal of persuasive authority, particularly those who are carefully chosen to address the specific needs of part-time faculty who are teaching adult students. They can introduce entirely new models and modes of thinking about teaching and learning that would be difficult for "insiders" to initiate. If they are among the cadre of major national figures in a given area, with notable publications in the field, their body of work can serve as the platform upon which continuing development initiatives can be built.

On the other hand, keynote speakers can be expensive, which can cut deeply into your development budget. Quality keynote speakers are sensitive to specific institutional needs. This should be part of an institution's evaluation of a potential candidate. If the speaker is not sensitive to these needs, and a keynote speech is a canned presentation, it can be less effective, unless the speech has a broad focus. A motivational speech is one example. Of lesser, but significant, concern is the time commitment for a workshop that leads off with a good keynote speech. Usually a full day is required, perhaps even twice per year, and that can represent half or more of the total time allotted at the institution.

Once the decision is made to utilize a keynote workshop, institutions are well advised to commit time to researching various candidates. Full-time faculty, especially a large and experienced one, can be of particular use here, since many of them would likely have encountered these speakers at national and regional conventions and could comment perceptively on their attributes. In any case, it is important to give whoever is chosen a clear set of expectations and goals for the workshop, since ambiguity will inevitably lead to disappointment. Both the institution and speaker bear responsibility in this area.

The Redlands Way

The Redlands Way was intended to establish a broad rubric under which all the development activities and their outcomes could be gathered. It is an organic concept, to be modified as the unit institution evolves. Abstracted, The Redlands Way is a way of conceiving professional development holistically. Its ultimate objective is to establish a substantial, well-trained group of adjunct faculty, with deeply established ties and commitments, who function as fully integrated faculty, or as "participatory" faculty, in the words of one accreditation agency. This means that adjuncts sit on committees, help shape curriculum, choose textbooks, conduct research with tenure track faculty, participate in governance to some extent, participate in graduation ceremonies, and possibly attend campus social events and gatherings. Their professional qualifications are up to date and relevant to the courses they teach, and they are academically well qualified. As a result, institutional investment gains a rich return in classroom excellence, a large body of participatory faculty on which to draw for conducting the business of the institution, student satisfaction, and the creation of a climate of satisfaction and collaboration that enriches the professional lives of institutional faculty, adjuncts, and most importantly, students.

The professional development program is one factor in this equation, but is by no means the only one. Several additional areas of effort and planning are implicit in the outcomes outlined above. Adjunct *curricula vitae* need to be examined closely, and strengths and weaknesses identified for development. Decisions need to be made about the level of institutional commitment to such professional enhancement. Will the institution assist adjuncts in attending conferences or acquiring additional professional and academic credentials? If so, at what level? If the institution does contribute to such development, what do they expect in return? If certain adjuncts are not well qualified and are unwilling to pursue additional training, will the institution retain them? For how long?

Another body that Redlands established was a Dean's Advisory Council, comprised of a dozen adjuncts representing various regions, programs, and disciplines. The semiannual workshops serve as the forum for the formal meeting of this group with the dean, but they are encouraged to communicate regularly by email and listserv as well. This body has direct input to the dean and is charged with making strategic and policy recommendations to the dean. This is another way that faculty can participate in support of the mission.

Regional Information Sessions

Regional information sessions can present a simple but effective faculty development option if an institution has satellite learning centers. In most institutions, adjunct faculty at learning centers teach their courses on a given night or nights, but don't appear to be invested. Such arrangements can have an isolating effect on faculty, and regional information sessions are an effective way to address this issue. They allow groups of faculty to assemble under a regional banner. They offer numerous advantages: faculty get to know each other personally (building a sense of community); issues specific to a center or region, such as facilities, student groups, staff, and support can be addressed collectively; communication about policies, rewards, and expectations can be efficiently covered; and a perception of regional linkage and commitment to the institutional mission can be reinforced.

Methodologies

We felt it important to model various teaching methods in our workshops and maximize the opportunities for adjuncts to actively participate in the sessions. Therefore, we used as many techniques as feasible. For some of the larger sessions, we began with a general presentation on a topic, followed by breakout sessions that were facilitated by full-time faculty. Some sessions were standard conference styles, with varying levels of interaction between presenters and audience, while others were highly informal and conversational in tone. A number of faculty presented case studies, while demonstrating effective methods in response to the cases presented. Various media were used, from overheads and PowerPoint to Blackboard e-learning platforms.

Results

Highlights

Six of these full day conferences have been offered and have attracted an average attendance of 95 faculty. Several key success factors have emerged.

- Offer a short overview of the topics and objectives, both for the day and sessions.

- Design breakouts of 10 to 15 faculty with guided but open discussion.

- Provide opportunities to compare conclusions or observations with other groups.

- Seek to build consensus on related topics to be explored.

- Publish and distribute breakout summaries to participants and faculty who are unable to attend.

These last two points provide possible threads to be picked up in future training. By performing these actions, the efforts extended and the objectives of the workshops are validated, and an opportunity is presented to build on that success through creating continuity and momentum.

Agendas

A standardized agenda format emerged through our experiences. It provides six hours of work time, not including customary opening remarks, luncheon, and break periods. A third of that work time is given to the plenary sessions on teaching effectiveness, student evaluation, classroom management, and similar topics. Another third is devoted to two iterations of concurrent sessions that include program road maps, discipline breakouts, and individual faculty skills enhancement through training in Blackboard and writing across the curriculum. The remaining time might include regional area meetings, mentor/mentee discussions, or administrative updates.

Participation

While 285 adjuncts have been invited to one or more of the six development conferences, the average number invited to any one conference gathering is 153. Participation rates averaged 62%, with a maximum of 85%.

We found unexpectedly that the attendance rate at the late August conferences is nearly 75% higher than the attendance rate at the early March gatherings.

Lessons Learned

A bounty of lessons have been learned from evaluating two full years of this development program. We discovered that some things didn't work very well. For example, using faculty pairs to facilitate the workshop breakouts led to some confusion. Many of the faculty lack professional training in facilitation, and the large groups of a dozen or more participants proved to be somewhat overwhelming. The case studies were less popular than many of the other activities, although the reason is not entirely clear. Other parts of the program were very popular, and will be built upon in subsequent trainings.

Adjunct Response to the Developmental Conference Program

We designed a simple assessment form that asked participants "to rate and comment on the relevance and/or helpfulness" of each conference segment. Using a 5–point Likert scale, the overall full day rating for each conference gathering tends to range from 4.20 to 4.35 with the exception of the first attempt (3.94) where we were plagued by overcrowded facilities and a closing segment that was poorly organized and unproductive. After four in-house conference gatherings, the fifth was turned over to an outside specialist for a daylong workshop called A Practical Workshop Introducing Ideas of Effective Teaching and Learning. The session was well received (4.35), and it stimulated the faculty to the point where the next conference gathering featured further discussion, exploration, and lab work on the keynote speaker's teaching techniques.

The more focused segments of the conferences such as program road maps, Blackboard training, and writing across the curriculum inevitably score high with the faculty. Well-presented information for faculty to use immediately in the classroom is always well received. These segments have been successful from the start, so we have continued to develop them with more advanced applications.

Accounting for Individual Differences

From the design phase, we were concerned about the great variance of teaching experience among participants. Could we develop meaningful sessions for adjuncts, regardless of their experience? To help answer this question, we asked participants to indicate on their assessment instrument the number of years they had taught at the University of Redlands. The responses were grouped into four subsections: 1) faculty with one year or less teaching at URSB, 2) faculty with one to two years, 3) faculty with three to five years, and 4) faculty with more than five years. Over the six conference sessions, faculty with more than five years comprised nearly forty per cent of the participants, approximately the same as groups 1 and 2 combined.

By calculating the overall conference rating for each experience level group, we hoped to identify any segment of faculty not being well served. Veteran faculty, for instance, had already addressed a number of these workshop topics earlier in their Redlands career. Findings from the first conference gathering supported this concern, with the overall rating by veterans substantially lower than that of the two groups of newer faculty. A deliberate effort was made to bring adjunct experience into the core of our various workshops, particularly in breakout sessions where their experiences were of great value to the relatively new faculty. In fact, the success of the Best Teaching Practices workshops was based on veteran faculty comments and their solutions to the problems posed. The two veteran subgroups comprise over 60% of conference participants and represent a resource that has proven invaluable in educating and influencing newer faculty. As we continued to rely on these adjuncts as point people in discussions and in other contexts, the difference in overall conference ratings among the four experience-level subgroups has been reduced by nearly 50%.

Not unexpectedly, the experience-level subgroup that consistently gives the gatherings its highest rating is group 2, faculty with one or two years in the classroom. We believe that this group is at least minimally acquainted with the system and the students. Many are now settling into a teaching style, and welcome pedagogical explorations and discussion of curricular coherence and education fundamentals. The newest faculty, group 1, however, gave the highest praise to our guest presenter, who walked everyone through the basics, from student learning styles to effective testing.

Ambiance

We spent a considerable amount of planning and effort on creating a conference gathering that was faculty-friendly and we hope, enjoyable. Good conference organization and staffing is a critical factor. From the opening of the registration desk to the cleanup of the closing reception, a responsible and accommodating presence can disarm even the most cynical faculty. The use of humor is also desirable. Some diversion during the luncheon period helps trigger informal conversation among previously unacquainted faculty members. Handouts are good, whether full sets of Power-Point slides, worksheets from breakouts, URSB coffee cups, or briefcases.

Agenda designers perceive 15-minute breaks between sessions as opportunities for the marginally committed adjunct to escape. Since each conference gathering has emphasized one major beneficial theme, we have found that providing an opportunity for talking to other faculty is invaluable. Make room for this, not just at the closing five minutes of the session, but in the beginning, middle, and the closing. Faculty frustration is greatest when a session is unable to reach its stated objectives because of faulty time management.

Be sure to include the attending staff and administrators, if any, as part of the opening introduction with praise for their contributions. Our assessment instrument asks for comments on all of the day's activities including the opening and closing remarks, which are most often made by administrators and program designers. The faculty ratings of these remarks tend to be below the overall ratings of the gathering. Clearly, a better job can be done on presenting the day's objectives and a review of achievements at the end of the program.

The facilities and organizational aspects, particularly presentation, have proven to be very important. Adjuncts expected a very professional experience, and the degree to which those expectations were met went a long way toward making them feel that their Saturdays had been well spent. It is clearly worth investing additional resources in materials.

Conclusion

To develop a successful adjunct faculty development plan—which by extension is also part of the full-time faculty professional development—faculty, administrators, and staff must establish comprehensive, mission-based goals for the plan. Without this broadly contextualized initiative, the plan will lack buy-in at crucial levels and will likely drift from its core purpose.

Once you've established a clear mission and set of goals, a broad group of stakeholders should enter the development conversation and assist in establishing constraints and opportunities. Extracting meaningful feedback from participants is crucial, and forms the foundation upon which subsequent sessions can be built. Gathering as much data as possible from the participants will pay dividends later on.

Pay close attention to support issues, such as how the program "feels" to a participant. One of the most encouraging comments we received during the training was from a notably cynical adjunct faculty member who commented that we were doing something right, because he didn't feel that we had wasted two of his Saturdays.

Does the development program really pay off? We certainly feel it does. Aside from the formal response data we have received, several anecdotal comments and reports have been encouraging. We've been told that none of our colleague institutions in the area offer anything approaching this level of development. That, in turn, has helped our faculty recruiting efforts, as adjuncts have told their colleagues about the quality program in place at Redlands. In addition, we are experiencing increased demand from the adjunct faculty for our teaching slots, as they commit themselves more fully to what they perceive to be a quality operation.

A dynamic faculty development program such as ours doesn't influence just the adjunct faculty. Indeed, the staff, administration, and faculty have collectively experienced a renewed commitment to, and understanding of, the mission and its role in the school.

We believe that institutions must construct meaningful faculty development programs to remain competitive and deliver on their educational promise to students. An engaging, useful, and practical development conference not only increases educational effectiveness, but positions an institution to achieve success as measured by many other standards as well.

9

Assuring Instructional Effectiveness

Walter Pearson

Assuring academic quality is central to the success of adult learning programs. Administrators for adult learning programs encounter multiple challenges that can often be simple to express but extremely complicated to do well. Getting the right students in the right classroom at the right time with the right instructor with the right books may sound simple, but budgets, staffing, course scheduling, publications, advertising, and program development are all the sorts of pressing issues that compete for the administrator's time.

Working to enhance academic quality is a top priority since adult students say that instructional effectiveness is the most important factor in assessing the college experience (Noel-Levitz, 2003). Each year, colleges and universities measure adult student opinion on a variety of topics using an instrument developed by the consulting firm Noel-Levitz. For the last five years instructional effectiveness has ranked highest in importance for adult students (see Table 9.1). This is logical, since adult students who study part-time are connected to the college almost entirely by their classroom experience.

This chapter will focus on ways administrators can help faculty enhance instructional effectiveness for adult learners. Faculty and students differ significantly in their perspectives about the meaning of instructional effectiveness. Both perspectives matter when building quality into your program. Faculty perceptions of quality in the academy include elevated expectations of student performance, level of preparation, and time on task (Schilling & Schilling, 1999). Adult students are attracted to an institutional commitment to excellence as they look for academic rigor and relevance, the use of clear and reasonable requirements, and flexibility.

TABLE 9.1

Importance of Instructional Effectiveness
using a Likert scale of 1–7

Year	4 year private	4 year public	2 year	Career and Private
2001–2002	6.32	6.29	6.14	6.22
2000–2001	6.32	6.28	6.14	6.27
1999–2000	6.35	6.30	6.14	6.30
1998–1999	6.35	6.31	6.17	6.34
1997–1998	6.37	6.31	6.19	6.32

Adapted from: Noel-Levitz (2003). *2003 national student satisfaction report.* Iowa City, IA: Author. Retrieved September 22, 2004, from http://www.noellevitz.com/pdfs/2003_SSI_Report.pdf

Factors that go into adult learners' judgment of instructional effectiveness include the instructor's competence as a leader in the learning process, knowledge of the subject, fairness in grading, timely feedback, accessibility, and care for the individual adult student (Noel-Levitz, 2003). Competent teachers of adults recognize that these learners appreciate building connections with other adult learners and connecting course knowledge with their lives (Dirkx, Kasworm, Graham, & Donaldson, 1999; Dirkx, Kasworm, Donaldson, & Graham, 2000).

Instructional effectiveness can be enhanced by four efforts: 1) supporting the induction of new faculty, 2) helping the faculty to become skillful instructors of adults, 3) monitoring teaching quality, and 4) recognizing and rewarding superior performance.

Since part-time faculty will probably teach a substantial number of courses in most adult learning programs, it is important to recognize the diversity within this category. Halfond (2000) cites the following categories:

- Moonlighters: typically have professional experience in a nonteaching field and a master's or J.D. degree

- Migrants: may be full-time faculty at another school, college, or university

- Apprentices: typically graduate students or all-but-dissertation students who hope to gain teaching experience

- Full-time wannabes (also known as road warriors): often Ph.D.s in the humanities with teaching experience who have not been able to find a full-time job in a saturated field

- Early and semi-retirees

You may wish to add another category to this list—loyalists: full-time faculty who are willing to teach in the evenings or on weekends. These groups vary in motivation, teaching skill, and experience. Your objective should be to create a common set of processes for all participants, using consistent induction, persistent and democratic faculty development, respectful monitoring and review, and an ongoing system of appreciation and recognition.

I will describe how we implement these processes and systems at Simpson College. The part-time students at this Midwestern, private liberal arts college are typical of the adult baccalaureate learners across the country (Pearson, 2000). However, they have registered satisfaction with instructional effectiveness at levels significantly above the national benchmark in the Noel-Levitz Adult Student Priorities Survey (2003). The key predictor of overall adult student satisfaction at Simpson has been the part-time student's agreement with the survey item, "There is a commitment to academic excellence at this institution." This confirms that the faculty who teach adult learners at Simpson College are performing at consistently high levels, leading to the question, "What are the systems that support that performance?"

New Faculty Induction

An induction process for new faculty increases awareness of the school's mission, goals, and expectations for both students and faculty. It may identify services available to students and faculty, the practice of andragogy, and any administrative expectations. The induction process starts with hiring, continues with an initial orientation, and proceeds into a phase of building connections with the institution.

Orientation

One key element of this induction process is the new faculty orientation. Each new instructor must attend an orientation even if the session has to be done individually to accommodate a single new hire. As the primary resource for the orientation, the Simpson faculty handbook contains the college's mission and articulates the vision and values of the faculty and staff in the adult learning program. The expectations for each class are implicit in the evaluation process form—an important part of this orientation that leads the candidate to understand how he or she will be evaluated and what expectations are inherent in the evaluation.

A set of student expectations is covered next. At Simpson, adult learners value quality, flexibility, convenience, and affordability. These expectations imply that faculty will accommodate makeup exams, seek to find the right combination of challenge and support for each student, and root course work in real problems (Keeton, Sheckley, & Griggs, 2002).

Identifying services for faculty and adult learners forms an important part of the orientation. New faculty members are acquainted with the electronic resources of the library and with how the library makes print materials available to off-campus faculty and students (students may check out a book on the phone and have it delivered to their home campus). The processes for academic support (free paper review and course tutoring) are explained. New instructors also become familiar with web course support and administrative technology that are available to them.

The topic of andragogy—the adult learner version of pedagogy—emphasizes the role of experience in learning, the value of discussion and experiential learning in course design and session construction, the need for flexibility in helping students to achieve the learning goals of the course, and the challenge of grade anxiety. A good instructor of adult learners integrates the students' experiences into the course design by engaging them in reflection on their experiences and connecting them with theory in a way that enables their knowledge to grow. Adult learners do not generally miss class for frivolous reasons, so instructors using best practices accommodate absences while keeping each student on track to meet the learning goals. Adult learners resist group projects unless the groups are kept small and the instructor sets aside class time and encourages electronic collaboration. Since adults often bring a great deal of fear or unrealistic expectations of their performance into the classroom, good instructors build confidence into the course early and use thoughtful grading practices that provide a wide variety of assessment options.

Each new part-time instructor receives a copy of *McKeachie's Teaching Tips* (McKeachie, 2002), that provides a wide range of well-researched ideas on teaching effectiveness. In addition, the participants view the collection of web-based teaching resources found on the Simpson website.

The final portion of the orientation deals with administrative processes such as payroll, expense reimbursement, clerical support, inclement weather policy, and attendance tracking required for federal financial aid. One ironclad rule stressed in this portion of the orientation is that no class session may be cancelled without notice to the office, because it is the office that contacts the students for any instructor absence.

Building Connections

The second stage of the induction process establishes a connection between the new hire and a full-time faculty member who has taught this course as well as other faculty teaching in the program. In a one-on-one session with a full-time faculty partner, ideas on syllabi and text choice are exchanged. At this time, the partner makes an appointment for a midterm observation of the new part-time faculty member. We have found that these sessions are often as valuable for the full-time faculty.

Persistent and Democratic Faculty Development

A collaborative approach to all faculty development is important for two reasons: it ensures that all sessions deal with the shared problems that faculty face, and it communicates the sense of respect that must exist for the many strong faculty members who teach in the adult program. By using surveys and dialog with groups of faculty to determine the agenda, we empower the faculty and the program is seen as relevant. Further collaboration is achieved with the use of faculty as panelists or session leaders in the program. Brockett (1991), Lawler and King (2000), and Moran (2001) provide a very important base for topics and best practices in faculty development.

Use these sessions as an opportunity for recognition as well. The location, food, and schedule should generate a covert message of appreciation and respect. Hold the session at a good hotel or in the best room on campus and order a nice meal. The event is enriched by setting up the room and designing the agenda to enhance discussion. Convey respect for busy faculty members by asking for input on the timing of the event and keeping it as short as possible.

Evaluate each development program in pursuit of continuous improvement. For instance, one lesson drawn from our evaluation process has been to provide regular discussion about departmental or discipline issues.

Clarity and Enthusiasm

Topics for faculty development should always include the nuts and bolts of quality instruction. Clarity and enthusiasm are the two key features common to effective instructors (Murray, 1983). Highly rated instructors typically build upon a foundation of clarity (by using examples, repetition, and stressing important points) and enthusiasm (through the use of humor and expressiveness). Metcalf and Cruickshank (1991) reviewed research that found that the following behaviors enable a faculty member to be clear:

- Orients, prepares students for what follows

- Provides standards, rules for satisfactory performance

- Teaches content step-by-step

- Uses a variety of teaching materials

- Demonstrates

- Provides examples and illustrations

- Communicates so that students understand

- Adjusts teaching to learners and topics

- Repeats and stresses directions and difficult points

- Causes students to organize materials in meaningful ways

- Provides practice

- Provides students with knowledge of how well they are doing

- Is task oriented

- Is verbally fluent

- Synthesizes what is taught and makes it relevant

- Provides students with opportunity to think about, respond to, and synthesize what they are learning

- Uses questions to assess student understanding

(p. 109)

In student evaluations, many instructors were rated high on clarity, but only the highest rated instructors combined clarity with enthusiasm. Examples of expressive behaviors include utilizing variation in voice, moving about within the room, using gestures, and making regular eye contact. These behaviors engage the students' attention, allowing other aspects of effective teaching to take hold in the classroom.

At Simpson, a wide variety of session topics has originated from these two key factors of clarity and enthusiasm. Further topics covered in recent sessions include the following titles.

Class Session Design

Not every instructor is good at keeping the learning structure of the course apparent to the students. One practice that provides greater clarity is to improve the structure of the class meeting. Bridging and recapitulation are important in making connections between prior and future sessions. Many of our instructors use a student-led summary of each session and recapitulation in the subsequent session. The same student opens the next session with a summary of what happened in the previous session. This practice contributes to the clarity of the materials and enables adult learners to become better students by reviewing their notes.

Another strategy in this regard is the use of an anticipatory and closing summary (Anticipatory summary: "Tonight we will cover . . ." Closing summary: "Tonight we covered . . ."). In this practice, the closing summary is often shifted to an assigned student who affirms and abridges the instructor's anticipatory summary.

Not all instructors are effective in using the text they assign. Students want to know that their average investment of $73 for the college text (National Association of College Stores, 2004) will help enhance their understanding of the course content. One tactic that many Simpson instructors now use is to assign a student to raise questions at the next class, based on the contents covered in the text. This primes the pump for a useful discussion that helps the students understand the important points in the text while allowing the instructor to more fully utilize the textbook.

Instructors who use these techniques in each session have reported that their students appear to understand the materials better. Their class meeting agenda might be something like this:

1) Check in and get started (a brief period).

2) Call on the assigned student who recaps the prior session (amplifying when needed).

3) Call on the "book questioner" (clarifying any questions or points raised).

4) Assign another student to recap this session.

5) Offer anticipatory summary of activities for the current class in the form of "Tonight we will cover...."

6) Proceed with the planned activity.

7) Wrap up with the student-led recap (instructor and other students provide support).

8) Assign a book questioner for next session while reminding students of readings and assignments.

9) Adjourn.

Grading Fairness

Grading makes many instructors feel uncomfortable. We have devoted sessions to sharing the research on student perceptions of grading fairly. In these, we've covered the implications for teaching practices, as well as the effective use of detailed paper assignments, review rubrics, and test construction. Houston and Bettencourt (1999) provide practices that influence student perceptions of fairness. They recommend:

• Interact with students respectfully, demonstrating a genuine concern for their outcomes.

• Whenever possible, exhibit flexibility in dealing with requests related to unusual circumstances.

- Provide some type of study guide or review to help students focus on important concepts.

- Test in a manner that is consistent with the presentation of the assigned material during the course.

- Carefully evaluate exams to ensure that students are not penalized by your oversights.

- Allow written, researched appeals to multiple-choice and essay test questions. (This provides students with an outlet and aids in their learning of the material and their ability to argue on their own behalf. It also helps the professor identify problems with clarity or content in exam questions.)

- Communicate with students to ensure that course policies are fully understood.

- "Market" course policies, particularly grade factors that are not typically evaluated.

- Recognize the impact of promptness in providing inputs (e.g., project guidelines) and/or feedback (e.g., comments on early drafts) on a student's subsequent performance.

- Take the time, to the degree possible, to allow students to discuss course grades.

Walvoord and Anderson (1998) and Speck (2000) provide additional resources for fair grading practices.

Other Topics

Most of our faculty development sessions have covered bread and butter topics such as Establishing a Good Classroom Climate, Providing Helpful Feedback, Improving Lectures, Leading Productive Discussion, and Designing Exercises That Enable Applications of Learning. Bligh (2000), Brookfield (1990), Heimlich and Norland (1994), and Vella (2000) have been important resources for these sessions. Recently, use of a course web site via WebCT has been added as a regular topic. Full- and part-time instructors who have effective practices in a particular area of teaching generally lead the sessions together. Occasionally, external experts such as Morris Keeton or a WebCT consultant have been brought in to share their expertise. In addition, library and audiovisual experts speak to acquaint faculty with new developments in classroom and library technology so that they can better serve adult learners.

Meetings by Academic Discipline

Annual departmental meetings between full-time faculty leaders and part-time faculty are a much-appreciated feature. They enable part-time faculty to stay plugged in to their department, have a voice in choosing texts, and interact on changes in curricula.

We also offer specialized groups of adjuncts more extensive meetings with appropriate full-time faculty. For instance, master teachers—area high school teachers who co-teach a senior-level content-specific teaching methods course with the full-time education faculty—benefit from these additional meetings.

Stream of Teaching Resources

The final element in faculty development for part-time faculty at Simpson College involves regular resource sharing. Faculty receive materials on enhancing teaching effectiveness from the college approximately every three weeks. These have included copies of articles from ERIC's Clearinghouse on Adult, Career, and Vocational Education, *The Teaching Professor,* and journal articles. This regular flow of ideas on teaching is designed to help everyone with self-reflection and to reinforce the notion that we take teaching effectiveness seriously at the college.

Monitoring and Recognizing Teaching Effectiveness

A comprehensive process of assuring instructional effectiveness requires observation, formative evaluation, summative evaluation, evaluation review and debriefing, appreciation, promotion, and recognition. Simpson College requires an observation of part-time faculty by senior full-time faculty in their first, fourth, and eighth course. Full-time faculty are compensated for performing their role which requires five steps:

1) Advance contact with the part-time faculty member

2) An observation (of not less than one hour) at a mutually agreed-upon time

3) The preparation of noninferential observations and a set of recommendations

4) Presentation of the report for discussion with the part-time faculty member

5) The submission of the final report

The discussions that take place in this process are often very useful to the new part-time faculty member but also serve to reassure all full-time faculty of the quality of the adult learning programs.

Student feedback during the course (formative evaluation) is an important way to build the connection between the teacher and learners. All faculty are encouraged to solicit periodic student feedback on the course before the end-of-term formal evaluation. We use a variety of student feedback approaches (Brookfield, 1995) to help faculty reflect upon and improve their courses.

Over time, and with enough students providing feedback, student evaluations of teaching can provide valid and useful information on teaching effectiveness (Aleamoni, 1987). At Simpson College, all students complete a one-page Likert scale teaching evaluation and one page of written comments for every course. Subsequently, instructors receive a copy of the written comments and a statistical summary that gives the class and term mean for a set of calculated factors and frequencies for each question. Most faculty need help in converting this statistical summary into a guide for decision-making. This review process also helps move instructors toward teaching excellence.

As these evaluation summaries are prepared for mailing, I conduct a careful review for each course. I attach personal notes of appreciation to those whose evaluation results are higher than the college mean and make a list of follow-up contacts for either new faculty or those whose evaluation results are below their normal pattern. For senior faculty with a long record of teaching excellence, these contacts take the form of a meeting over coffee or lunch to express our appreciation and to ask directly what they feel happened in the class.

For new faculty, my role is to listen. This seems to be what each new person needs the most. Teaching can be lonely and frustrating at times. Having an experienced person listen and help talk through a class, either to praise or to solve problems, has proven helpful in supporting growth among instructors. The evaluation summary sometimes provides clear guidance—strengthen lectures, come to class ready, choose a different book—but sometimes the answers to the problems may be murky. There is science in teaching. There are clear principles that provide broad guidance. However, teaching is also an art. Helping the newer instructor achieve balance between those principles and her or his own style can probably only be achieved through dialogue.

One example might prove useful. Simpson has two full-time faculty who teach only for the adult learning program. For one of these faculty members, who teaches in a technical field, the first year of teaching was very difficult. The teaching load consisted of two courses each 10-week term, and each course was a new preparation in the first year. Student evaluations and colleague observations reported a lack of organization and many signs of stress. Each term we sat down to review the evaluation summary and the student comments before mapping out further suggestions. In addition, we recruited a highly–rated adult learning teacher to serve as an individual coach. The second year saw many changes in the course content and process, but the evaluation results were only marginally higher and brought many more (often unpleasant) meetings to seek further improvements. By the third year, there were no signs of stress, and evaluation results were markedly improved. In the spring of the third year, this instructor was selected by the students as "adult educator of the year" in balloting conducted by the Alpha Sigma Lambda (ASL) chapter. Focusing on teaching effectiveness, consistent feedback, coaching, and problem solving made a difference.

Recognizing Teaching Effectiveness

At many campuses, the ASL chapter helps in the process of recognizing teaching effectiveness by conducting a ballot for the award of "adult educator of the year." At Simpson College this award is formally presented at the ASL induction ceremony in the spring and the award recipient is invited to give a lecture on a topic of his or her choice. The award winner is featured in the employee newsletter and the adult student newsletter, we put his or her picture in the catalog and name on a plaque maintained in the office. Schools often use variations in their approach to faculty recognition. At Baldwin-Wallace College, for instance, the recipient is asked to submit a brief description of his or her philosophy or strategies for teaching effectiveness. These teaching ideas are incorporated into the faculty handbook. Recognition of superior performance is always an important way to sustain excellence.

Another element in a comprehensive system for recognizing teaching effectiveness is a promotion process. Most colleges have thoughtful methods of regulating the promotion process for full-time faculty. However, a parallel process for part-time faculty is needed as well. At Simpson, part-time faculty who have taught for at least three years and at least eight courses are eligible for consideration for promotion to lecturer, a position that carries a higher salary, payment for travel time, reimbursement for mileage, a modest professional development fund, first bid for open courses, and invitations to process with full-time faculty at convocations and graduation. Full-time faculty must have conducted at least three observations of the prospective lecturer, and the respective department chair must recommend the promotion. During a final meeting with the candidate, I review the candidate's record and express appreciation before forwarding the file to the Faculty Personnel Committee, which acts on the recommendation to promote. The college gains from this process by cementing a long-term relationship with a talented teacher.

While there is never enough money for everything that matters, increasing salaries and giving gifts annually is another way to express the appreciation of the institution. To full-time wannabes, the compensation can never be enough. For moonlighters, the money is not the most important aspect of their relationship with teaching. No matter what their orientation, we believe we owe them as much as we can afford. Regular and consistent efforts to raise the compensation (in the 5% range) in recent years have moved the institution toward fairness. Other schools may offer other incentives. For instance, enabling access to tuition remission on a proportional basis is another benefit that Drury University has provided to its adjunct faculty.

An imprinted holiday gift that is given annually to everyone who has taught during the year is another symbolic way of expressing appreciation to part-time faculty at Simpson College. This gift has taken the form of a sweater, a travel mug, a pen, a briefcase, or a portfolio. Care is taken to engage all staff in delivering these gifts personally with a direct expression of thanks.

Lessons Learned

Induction of New Faculty

- Make expectations clear
- Build connection to experienced faculty
- Provide practical resources

Faculty Development

- Use persistent and democratic process
- Build in recognition and appreciation
  - Involve current faculty as leaders
  - Remember that location, schedule, and food connote respect
- Focus on practical ideas to address real problems
- Bring in current research

Monitor Quality

- Review all evaluation results
- Utilize peer observation
- Debrief in problem classes
- Listen

Recognition and Appreciation

- Write notes to superior performers
- Present annual awards
- Provide holiday gifts
- Seek annual salary increases and expand benefits
- Create promotion process with real rewards

Summary

A focus on enhancing instructional effectiveness can pay very large dividends. A solid system of induction for new faculty enables long-term success. Persistent and democratic faculty development sustains motivation and supports student achievement and satisfaction. Consistent monitoring and feedback help faculty through discouraging events even as they defend and convey the importance of academic excellence. Finally, recognition and appreciation enhance motivation and instructional effectiveness.

References

Aleamoni, L. (1987). Typical faculty concerns about student evaluation of teaching. In L. M. Aleamoni (Ed.), *New directions for teaching and learning: No. 31. Techniques for evaluating and improving instruction* (pp. 25–31). San Francisco, CA: Jossey-Bass.

Bligh, D. A. (2000). *What's the use of lectures?* San Francisco, CA: Jossey-Bass.

Brockett, R. G. (Ed.). (1991). *New directions for adult and continuing education: No. 51. Professional development for educators of adults.* San Francisco, CA: Jossey-Bass.

Brookfield, S. D. (1990). *The skillful teacher.* San Francisco, CA: Jossey-Bass.

Brookfield, S. D. (1995). *Becoming a critically reflective teacher.* San Francisco, CA: Jossey-Bass.

Dirkx, J. M., Kasworm, C., Donaldson, J. F., & Graham, S. W. (2000). *The experiences of adult undergraduate students—What shapes their learning?* Paper presented at the annual meeting of the American Educational Research Association, New Orleans, LA. (ERIC Document Reproduction Service No. ED440275)

Dirkx, J. M., Kasworm, C., Graham, S. W., & Donaldson, J. F. (1999). *Adult undergraduates' participation and involvement: Future directions for theory and research.* Paper presented at the annual meeting of the American Educational Research Association, Montreal, Canada. (ERIC Document Reproduction Service No. ED430473)

Halfond, J. (2000). When adjunct faculty are in the majority: Focusing on those who make us what we are. *Continuing Higher Education Review, 64,* 47–55.

Heimlich, J. E., & Norland, E. (1994). *Developing teaching style in adult education.* San Francisco, CA: Jossey-Bass.

Houston, M., & Bettencourt, L. (1999). But that's not fair! An exploratory study of student perceptions of instructor fairness. *Journal of Marketing Education, 21*(2), 84–96.

Keeton, M., Sheckley, B., & Griggs, J. (2002). *Effectiveness and efficiency in higher education for adults: A guide for fostering learning.* Dubuque, IA: Kendall/Hunt.

Lawler, P. A., & King, K. P. (2000). *Planning for effective faculty development: Using adult learning strategies.* Malabar, FL: Krieger.

Metcalf, K., & Cruickshank, D. (1991). Can teachers be trained to make clear presentations? *Journal of Educational Research, 85*(2), 107–117.

McKeachie, W. J. (2002). *McKeachie's teaching tips: Strategies, research, and theory for college and university teachers* (11th ed.). Boston, MA: Houghton Mifflin.

Moran, J. (2001). *Collaborative professional development for teachers of adults.* Malabar, FL: Krieger.

Murray, H. (1983). Low-inference classroom teaching behaviors and student ratings of college teaching effectiveness. *Journal of Educational Psychology, 75*(1), 138–149.

National Association of College Stores. (2004). *Higher education retail market facts & figures 2004.* Oberlin, OH: Author. Retrieved September 22, 2004, from http://www.nacs.org/public/research/higher_ed_retail.asp

Noel-Levitz (2003). *2003 national adult student priorities report.* Iowa City, IA: Author. Retrieved September 22, 2004, from http://www.noellevitz.com/pdfs/2003_ASPS_Report.pdf

Pearson, W. (2000). Enhancing adult student persistence: The relationship between prior learning assessment and persistence toward the baccalaureate degree (Doctoral dissertation, Iowa State University, 2000). *Dissertation Abstracts International, 61,* 3025.

Schilling, K. M., & Schilling, K. L. (1999). Increasing expectation for student effort. *About Campus, 4*(2), 4–7.

Speck, B. (2000). *Grading students' classroom writing* (ASHE-ERIC Higher Education Report, 27[3]). Washington, DC: George Washington University, Graduate School of Education and Human Development. (ERIC Document Reproduction Service No. ED440602)

Vella, J. (2000). *Taking learning to task: Creative strategies for teaching adults.* San Francisco, CA: Jossey-Bass.

Walvoord, B. E., & Anderson, V. J. (1998). *Effective grading: A tool for learning and assessment.* San Francisco, CA: Jossey-Bass.

Part IV

Technological Applications

10

The Role of Distance Education in Enhancing Accessibility for Adult Learners

Karen I. Rhoda

Advances in technology have transformed the way in which the academy offers its curricula. Colleges and universities have applied these advancements to distance education. This enables students to enroll in courses and complete degree programs that are offered online, by CD-ROM, or in studios through ISPN lines or IP video. Most institutions of higher education have concentrated their efforts on the conversion of their face-to-face courses to an online format. It is this delivery mechanism, offered in an anytime, anywhere virtual classroom, that has attracted increasing numbers of students. The student population that took online courses in 1998 numbered 710,000. More than two million students enrolled in online courses in 2002. This four-year period reflects a 36% increase in student enrollment in online higher education.

When other forms of distance education are included, the number of students enrolling in distance education courses and degree programs increases even more. The U.S. Department of Education released its findings from a survey conducted in the spring of 2002. The survey, which had a 94% response rate, included 1,600 degree-granting institutions across the United States, and reported that "enrollment in college-level distance courses—classes taught online or remotely through audio or video feeds—jumped from 1.3 million to 2.9 million between 1997–98 and 2000–01" (Giegerich, 2003, p. 1). The survey indicated that the number of online courses offered by the academy more than doubled in the three-year time period between 1997 and 2000, from 47,500 to 118,000 classes. Ninety percent of the online courses were provided in an asynchronous environment, with 85% of two- and four-year institutions of higher education offering enrollment in online courses.

As the opportunity for students to complete courses—indeed, entire degrees—online continues to increase in the years to come, it is important to understand how the academy is structuring its organization to provide for this new approach in higher education. This chapter addresses the ways in which institutions of higher education 1) seek to understand how best to build an infrastructure that offers courses and degree programs in an anytime, anywhere environment, and 2) may develop policies and procedures to serve the students who seek higher education via distance education.

It is clear that the current era in higher education is unlike any other for colleges and universities. The use of technology to reach students electronically is vital for institutions, as societal processes continue to step up the pace for the lives of most people. Many adult learners who seek higher education cannot commute to campuses in the same way as traditional students. Today's lifestyles demand flexibility for potential students to be able to fit higher education into their busy lives. As Weigel (2002), notes:

> The twenty-first century is a time of unparalleled promise for higher education. Mass-produced distance education will open up new knowledge horizons for millions of people who otherwise would have no opportunity to attend a college or university, and blended approaches to elearning will enrich classroom-based education. It would be difficult to imagine a more creative or rewarding era for educators. (p. 127)

A growing number of institutions of higher learning rely on the revenue produced from distance education delivery. Today, universities and colleges compete not only for the student enrollments on campus but also for those students who enroll in online courses and programs. Instead of commuting or traveling to a college or university for face-to-face courses, a student is only a click away from a wide variety of courses and degree programs at a wide range of tuition rates. Indeed, students are able to "shop for courses that best accommodate their schedules and learning styles, and then transfer the credit to the university where they will earn their degrees" (Howell, Williams, & Lindsay, 2003, p. 2).

The tuition revenue garnered from online delivery of courses and degree programs has steadily increased and will continue to do so for those institutions making a commitment to this form of education and to the students who seek it. In 2001 the revenue produced for distance education stood at $4.5 billion. Its production is projected to increase to $11 billion in 2005 (as cited in Gould, 2003).

It is not only the revenue to be gained that propels this form of education. Those in higher education—especially public institutions—respond to the dictate to educate humanity and improve societal conditions. In response to the democratic principle to provide educational opportunity for all, administrators of higher education, and also legislators who control funding for education, note the expanded access to higher education that distance education provides for many individuals. Particularly in states in where degree completion lags, access to higher education via online learning presents the hope that greater numbers of the citizenry will pursue and complete a college degree. Indeed, increased access to higher education as a shared value can help attract industry and business to a geographic region.

This makes the work exciting and energizing for those of us involved in distance education programs. It also demands that we focus attention on the needs of the types of learners best served by online courses and degree programs. Careful strategic planning is required to create and maintain excellence for the student population enrolled in distance education programs. This requires knowing how to organize distance education services on a campus, especially in the current economic environment of scarce financial resources.

The Advantages of Increased Access to Higher Education

At a time when the academy is applying advanced technology to higher education, 11 million adult learners in the United States are seeking a college degree. They pursue an education in a society in which a college degree—in some cases an advanced degree—has become critical to compete in the employment arena as jobs change, entire occupations are eliminated, and new ones develop. Their lifestyle is better accommodated by the advantages of the virtual classroom, where they are not constrained by having to fit their schedule to rigid times or locations. Adult learners often can't fit the pursuit of a college degree into their busy schedule. Retention of these students is difficult, when they must contend with limited parking spaces and long walks across campus in all types of weather to a classroom furnished with uncomfortable chairs.

Adult learners' schedules tend to be filled with the demands of an occupation, household tasks, family obligations, and childcare responsibilities. Some adult learners travel for their job, are involved in community tasks, are single parents, and may even juggle all of the above and two or more jobs to make ends meet. But for today's adult learners, higher education is also as close as their computer. It is therefore not surprising that students who report participation in distance education tend to be those who are employed and have family responsibilities (U.S. Department of Education, 2002). Online degree seekers tend to include more women then men. These students seek the flexibility and convenience of online degree programs that allow them to balance their schedule and still pursue a college degree.

This flexibility means that some students are able to increase their course load and graduate sooner while reducing their childcare expenses and eliminating the need to travel to and from campus. Imagine the relief of the parent who can stay home with children after working all day, still be enrolled in college, and not need to pay for additional childcare. There is no inclement weather in the virtual classroom. Visualize having laundry in the washer or dryer, being clothed in flannel pajamas and wooly socks on a cold winter's night, and being able to be online in the virtual classroom, working in a discussion group with the professor and fellow students. Visualize walking directly from one's computer to the kitchen to pack school lunches for the next day rather than plodding across a dark campus on icy sidewalks to a snowy parking lot to climb into one's cold car for the ride home.

It is not only the adult learner who seeks the convenience and flexibility of distance education in the pursuit of a college degree. Bash (2003), Cureton (2003) and Oblinger (2003) describe the traditional student lifestyle as no longer characterized by being able to concentrate only on college courses and the collegiate social scene. Many traditional age students exhibit nontraditional lifestyles very much like those of the adult learner. Students who enter college directly from high school and in the years just afterward (especially those entering urban universities in metropolitan locations) reflect the following patterns:

- They work up to 40 hours or more per week to pay for tuition, books, and living expenses. All of these costs increase each year they remain in school.

- They view their education as a means to improve their economic circumstances following graduation.

- They experience anxiety about the price of their education and their future careers.

- They expect institutions of higher education to operate with timeliness in the provision of service and information.

- They may live in dorms or apartments and take online courses. Johnstone, Ewell, and Paulson (2002) report that at one land-grant university, on-campus students make up 85% of its distance education population.

Traditional age students are more like adult learners than students in any previous era. Both groups seek the convenience and flexibility of distance education courses and degree programs in order to cope with their busy schedules and graduate in a timely manner.

Traditional age students have grown up with technology, so they are comfortable communicating in the online environment. Picture the following, as Cureton (2003) did in her keynote address for the WebCT User Conference attendees: students sitting in their dorms, online in a chat room on their computer, headphones on and listening to a CD, with Palm Pilot and cell phone at hand. It is not a surprise to learn that "the younger the age group, the higher is the percentage who use the Internet for school, work, and leisure" (Oblinger, 2003, p. 38). Both traditional age students and adult learners are aware that more education leads to better paying occupations, so they are motivated by this monetary goal to perform well in classes. They know that income increases with more education. In fact, average family earnings, based on the educational attainment of the householder, are almost twice as much for the person earning a bachelor's degree ($96, 016) as for the person earning a high school diploma ($52,252) (Bash, 2003).

Distance Education: Its Effective Administration

As the technology of distance learning has enabled the offering of online degree programs, "transformational leaders in [distance] education must be capable of helping its stakeholders (e.g., administrators, faculty, students, trustees), recognize that there are obvious benefits in doing business in new ways" (Beaudoin, 2003, p. 10). Distance education "leaders can capitalize on their institution's growing need to remain competitive in a broader arena, by demonstrating how distance education offerings, once relegated to the margins, can be central to an institution's strategic planning for success" (Beaudoin, 2003, p. 10). A growing number of administrators are recognizing that distance education has increased the pace at which their faculty members have embraced technology. As noted earlier, for many institutions this has resulted in enrollments among students who could not attend face-to-face classes.

A systematized process of operation is needed to effectively administer a growing number of online course and degree program offerings to an ever greater number of students from an expanding geographic area. Verduin and Clark (1991) emphasize the need for a specific model in order to generate success in distance learning programs, and Scollin and Tello (1999) point to the framework for understanding the administrative and academic issues necessary for success in distance learning. Drawing on that paradigm, success in distance education programs is best structured by means of a centralized operation for effective provision of services.

Within that centralized structure, technical support and training for faculty, comprehensive student services, and network/server infrastructure must be integrated into an effective entity. In fact, the Higher Learning Commission of the North Central Association of Colleges and Schools (2002) notes that this integration is critical to meet the accreditation criteria for the "best practices for electronically offered degree and certificate programs" (p. 52). Concentration on this integration promotes good teaching, effective learning, and the broadening of students' intellectual horizons. Best practice focuses on strategies that produce quality courses and student services, rather than on technology alone.

Student Services for Distance Education Students

For example, student services professionals in distance education do not see the online students. Therefore, the offering of online courses and degree programs adds a layer of complexity to the services typically provided for students enrolled in on-campus courses and degree programs. Services for students who enroll in distance education need to be designed carefully with the realization that students may never come to campus. Careful guidance of students helps build an affinity between the students and the college or university.

The Factors to Consider

Experience provides clear evidence that high-quality, comprehensive student support services are critical to enrollment and retention for online degree programs. Access to education in a digitized society confirms that services for online learners must provide the vital link that produces affinity between the student and the academic campus. For today's learners, especially adults, this means the expectation for responsiveness to their individual needs. This kind of response to adult students represents a departure of service for most traditional universities. Services for adults in online programs must be "concerned largely with changing procedures and processes to better serve new audiences. The changes have been highly entrepreneurial, market oriented and responsive to these growing [numbers] of [students]" (Hanna, 2003, p. 69). As Cureton (2003) points out, today's adult learners come to the academy from the work arena expecting the same quick response they get from an ATM machine.

As noted, traditional age students have grown up in a technological era, comfortable communicating in online chat rooms, surfing the Internet for information and using email, Palm Pilots, cell phones, and instant messaging. Many adult students have become accustomed to relying on technology because of their experience in the work arena. However, this doesn't mean that all traditional students and adult learners will know how to take an online course and will have a positive attitude toward doing so. Several factors need to be remembered.

- Adult students beginning or returning to college may not have experience with the kind of technology that is applied to higher education. Many enroll in college studies to help them enter the professional or white-collar work arena from their current blue-collar status. They may know how to operate a robotic piece of equipment but may not know how to navigate their way through course management software such as WebCT. Though the baby boomers surf the web more than any other age group (Winters, 2000), they may not have acquired the technical skills required to be students in online classes.

- Lifestyles today reflect such high use of technology that "approximately 90% of adult students have access to a computer—either at home or in the workplace" (Bash, 2003, p. 47). However, this does not remove the trepidation of adult learners who are grappling with technology, academic jargon, and the unfamiliar process of taking college courses while trying to maintain their work and family responsibilities. Some adult learners begin or return to college because their place of work has downsized or changed ownership. Adult learners who are without jobs and are unnerved about their personal situation are already feeling vulnerable. This feeling is compounded when they must attempt to deal with technology as applied to collegiate learning.

- Student services for distance learning programs are typically set up for all students who enroll in online courses and degree programs. Students run the gamut from highly sophisticated computer users to those who need help with the simplest technology. Since the digital divide is widening rather than narrowing, it has resulted in economic barriers to technological proficiency. This impedes the ability to succeed in the technology in collegiate settings, particularly in state universities with open admission policies.

- Distance education programs have greater success in recruiting and retaining students when their operation includes student services. Programs that don't have student services are more likely to fail. Schrum (as qtd. in "Helping Students Become Tech-Savvy," 2003) notes, "colleges seem to have this sink or swim mentality when it comes to [comfort levels with technology]. It's like, 'sign up for these courses and we'll see if you make it'" (p. 3).

- Accreditation for distance education programs that are offered entirely online requires that student services be part of the criteria. For example, the Higher Learning Commission of the North Central Association of Colleges and Schools provides an extensive list of best practices for student services in order to acquire accreditation for electronically offered degree and certificate programs in the region under its auspices. Institutions must heed these guidelines if they want to receive accreditation and be able to recruit students by promoting this credential.

Student Services That Build Successful Programs

Certainly, if "students are taking the adventure with us; it's our place to make sure they get the services they need" (Rhoda qtd. in Lorenzetti, 2002, p. 1). A fundamental element for success in a distance learning operation is remembering that students are enrolled in these courses and degree programs so that they do not need to come to campus. However, many students enroll in distance education and also in traditional (face-to-face) classes in the same semester. They do so for these reasons:

- They desire/require flexibility in their schedule.

- They are able to enroll in more credit hours per term and thus graduate sooner.

- They have to enroll as a full-time student to meet financial aid requirements.

- They may need to enroll in both traditional and distance education courses in order to complete their degree program, because not all courses for the degree program of their choice may be offered as fully online courses.

Many adult learners have accumulated credit hours at various institutions of higher learning, and this pattern can be expected to increase with the availability of distance education. Johnstone, Ewell, and Paulson (2002) described this trend, reporting that "58 percent of those ultimately earning baccalaureate degrees [in 1999] had attended two or more institutions, while 19 percent attended three or more" (p. 1). Students of all ages "swirl," that is, they enroll at more than one institution at the same time.

In addition, many campuses offer traditional (face-to-face) classes that are web assisted. These classes enhance traditionally scheduled courses. Savvy higher education administrators are directing their institutions to utilize one course management system (e.g., WebCT) for both web-assisted and distance education courses as part of their strategic planning. In the tough budgetary conditions that schools continue to encounter, this efficient use of a single system is cost- and time-effective, since it requires less learning of the course management format for both faculty and students and also less use of server space and technical management.

Leaders in the operation of student services for distance education need to instill guiding philosophical principles for staff members that build the student's affinity with the institution of higher learning and set a standard that reinforces that every student deserves their very best efforts. These philosophical principles should be the foundation for student services in distance education. A quality distance education program should provide the following elements:

- A comprehensive web site that is continually updated with revisions and current information that includes email links for faculty teaching online courses and the distance education staff.

- A generic email link on the web site so that a student's message can be received even if a staff member is out of the office.

- A link to distance education from the institution's home page.

- Online admission, registration, and tuition payment.

- Course catalogs that are readily available by mail and online at the program's web site.

- Same business day responses to online and phone inquiries.

- A student information letter that includes ID, password, and logon instructions mailed to each student before the start of a new term, with an online example of the same provided on the web site.

- Same business day responses to students' questions, problems, and concerns ranging from admission and registration questions to ones about technical difficulties. Every question should be considered important, and information should be repeated as frequently as needed. Each student should be warmly greeted and responded to in a positive manner whether by email or on the phone.

- A tech help desk operated during regular business hours as well as evenings and weekends, seven days a week.

- A web-based help and support area complete with frequently asked questions (FAQs).

- A toll-free telephone number.

- An online orientation in how to take an Internet course, complete with exercises in email, explanations about chat rooms, netiquette, and practice exams.

- Help with adding a course within the appropriate time period once the term is underway.

- Referral to college program offices for academic advising and follow-up that contact has been established.

- Online tutoring and advice from the campus's writing center.

- Applicable course orientation and e-learning software shipped to students' homes.

- Online library services with provision of journal articles that are emailed to students and books that are shipped with the label affixed for their return shipment at no charge.

- Online ordering of textbooks from the campus bookstore and shipping of textbooks and course software directly to students' homes.

- Recording and tracking of all inquiries.

- Ongoing training for new student service staff and also for any staff or student worker who is the first point of inquiry for a student.

- Assessment of student services.

A very important point needs to be made about training the tech help support staff. These employees must be carefully trained and their work needs to be continually monitored and reviewed. Undergraduate or graduate students may be employed for this work, but if they are, new student employees will need to be trained as their classmates graduate. Tech help support is vital. These employees, working after regular office hours and on weekends, communicate by phone and email with students having technical difficulty. However, students also have nontechnical questions after regular hours, so these workers also need to be able to answer basic questions about admission, registration, and obtaining textbooks. For instance, the add/drop period after classes begin is a critical time during which students need to be retained. Distance education administrators should consider having the full-time student services staff work after 5:00 p.m. during the add/drop time period. This enables oversight of the tech help support replies to students' questions and results in more effective retention of students. Furthermore, questions asked on weekends, when students are trying to study online, cannot wait until Monday.

Simply providing online courses and degree programs is not sufficient to stimulate significant enrollment growth even when coupled with comprehensive services. The enhanced flexibility and convenience of distance education must be marketed extensively and targeted to the appropriate potential students. Distance education programs do well when aggressively promoted in local, regional, and national media (e.g., newspapers, radio, television, web sites, and college guides).

The lesson here is that these services can be built as the distance education program grows but services must keep pace with rising enrollment in order to sustain the growth. It is important to remember that another university is just a click away.

Offering College Curricula Online

The hallmark of offering higher education courses and degree programs online is the flexibility of anytime and anywhere access. This flexibility of access that has become so attractive to adult learners allows institutions of higher education to recruit students outside of their typical commuter area and collaborate with other institutions to offer online degree programs. Nonetheless, many institutions of higher education have been struggling with the transformation of their delivery of higher education from the traditional classroom setting to the online arena.

The ability to offer college-level courses and entire degree programs via the technology of distance learning has brought change to the organizational structure of higher education as well as to the very processes of pedagogical/andragogical models. The conversion of material delivered in the classroom's face-to-face setting to material for web delivery is challenging and causes faculty to rethink their teaching methodology. The best taught online courses engage learners in productive learner-centered courses so that learning outcomes are equivalent to those in the traditional classroom.

In many institutions of higher learning, administrators have watched enrollment in their distance learning programs grow. This is the direct result of the hard work of leaders in these programs and the willingness of dedicated faculty members to develop and teach online courses. Students have continued to enroll even as cautionary rhetoric in academia has rumbled that "the quality of these offerings would always be inferior to that of face-to-face instruction" (Allen & Seaman, 2003, p. 3). Meanwhile, the faculty teaching online courses and their students have indicated that online learning provides in-depth, well-researched chat room discussions with a greater sense of knowledge about relevant topics. They also note that communication with fellow students from a breadth of diverse backgrounds takes place more than in the traditional classroom. Faculty report that their communication with students in their virtual classrooms is more academically enriching than in their traditional classroom. Students report that more content is delivered in the online course than in the same course taught in the traditional classroom. The online students learn this from fellow students who are taking the same course but in the traditional manner—perhaps taught by the same professor. This is likely when faculty post the same course content to a web site that they intend to cover in the traditional course but run out of time to cover in the face-to-face setting. In spite of these reports, "the belief that online learning is of lower quality" (Allen & Seaman, 2003, p. 3) continues as does the notion that those students participating in these educational experiences do so because they have no time to do otherwise.

Another myth is that online courses are easier than courses in the traditional classroom, despite indications from students that, if anything, these courses are more difficult and certainly more time-consuming. This is seldom a problem for adult learners, since they expect and even thrive on learning challenges, whether in the traditional or virtual classroom.

Research indicates that academic performance shows no significant difference; in fact, there is "a remarkable consistency of results in studies dating to the early 1970s" (Bates, 2000, p. 199) when distance education courses are compared to traditionally taught ones. Diaz (2002) points out that adult students have higher GPAs than their younger classmates in the traditional and also in the virtual classroom.

Technology is not put to its most effective use when course delivery focuses on simply reproducing course material as it is delivered in the traditional classroom. It is far better to understand the processes that technology can contribute to teaching and learning, and the interaction and interchange that technology is able to bring to the learning experience of the adult students sitting at computers in their homes. What needs to be studied in greater detail is how technology can best be applied to produce optimal learning outcomes. That is, which part of a course should be delivered as video streaming, which should be audio, which should be a chat room discussion, and how can we maximize the writing of papers? This is what is done in a well-managed instructional design session. The technology available to use for distance education continues to become more advanced each year, which gives educators the opportunity to produce ever more engaging virtual classrooms for students.

As student enrollment in virtual classrooms increases, online education gains credibility regarding its delivery of a quality educational experience. In a Sloan Consortium survey, presidents and chief academic officers in higher education were asked about the quality of their institutions' online courses and degree programs.

> When asked to compare learning outcomes in online courses with those for face-to-face instruction, academic leaders put the two on very close terms today, and expect the online offerings to continue to get better relative to the face-to-face option. A majority of academic leaders (57 percent) already believe that the learning outcomes for online education are equal to or superior to those of face-to-face instruction. (Allen & Seaman, 2003, p. 3)

At the same time, the point needs to be made that not all courses are suited to online delivery, and not all faculty wish to learn the processes for teaching in this manner. Furthermore, not all students are suited to online learning—some would be better served if they enroll in traditional courses that provide face-to-face instruction. Academic success in online courses requires motivation, self-discipline, good time management skills, and the ability to communicate well in an online environment.

Producing Quality Online Courses

The focus in this section is on support for faculty in creating online courses for students so that their learning outcomes are equivalent to those in the traditional classroom. It does not touch upon what drives faculty behavior or how support for faculty should be set up for teaching and learning endeavors other than that for distance education on campuses. For those topics I refer readers to the book *Managing Technological Change* (Bates, 2000).

It is important for adult learners to know that their learning objectives will be met when they enroll in online degree programs. They are concerned and vocal about receiving a worthwhile educational experience for their tuition dollars. This does not imply, however, that the learning journey should be dictated by student satisfaction. Rather, faculty should guide and monitor the collegiate learning experience and conferring of academic degrees.

Institutional Policies: The Guidance of Distance Education

Institutional policies related to distance education courses and instruction have been implemented in many colleges and universities. In some schools a standing committee of administrators and faculty has been formed to provide advice to the distance education program. These committees often create policies and procedures regarding online courses and degree programs.

There must be a procedure for providing information about what courses and degree programs will be offered. This information guides the process for the establishment of online courses. Online courses and degree programs must be monitored and guided by the faculty as a whole with the aim of designing courses that are appropriate to the rigor and breadth of the collegiate level.

Decisions about distance education courses and degree programs should be initiated within academic departments in the same manner as traditional courses and degree programs. Courses and degree programs should be chosen to meet the institution's strategic planning and objectives. Departmental curriculum committees need to carefully deliberate about whether it is appropriate to convert courses to a web-based format. As the distance education program continues to expand, it is critical that current degrees continue to be regimented and systematized. Each institution of higher education needs to design and adopt its own system to monitor these issues, and of course, evaluate its online courses.

Faculty designing online courses need to be provided with comprehensive technical support and training. It is a mistake to require faculty to independently learn the technology necessary to develop an online course. It is far more productive and cost effective for the institution if faculty are able to concentrate only on the content that will be converted to the online format. As Bates (2000) indicates, "The highest cost in teaching and learning is instructor or subject expert time" (p. 26).

Providing "comprehensive and systematic technical and professional support for faculty" (Bates, 2000, p. 105) within the structure of a centralized distance education office is far more cost effective for the institution than adding the expense of training faculty in the use of every technology used to produce online courses. In this model, it is the task of the distance education office to provide faculty with instructional designers who utilize cutting-edge technology and are versed in current learning research. While faculty decide what tools to apply to their course content in conference with instructional designers, the design team completes the digital art, video streaming, embedded audio, and links to other web sites.

The employment of instructional designers and assistants trained in digital art must be sized to the number of courses being taught each semester and the number of new courses being developed. Previously designed courses should be updated to keep the content current as new technology is adopted. Institutions need to take the approach that faculty don't need to be "techies." Schools should provide them support "in the range of one technical support person to every twenty to thirty full-time instructors using technology" (Bates, 2000, p. 106). It is the task of instructional designers to bring the faculty's teaching proficiency and knowledge base to the web-based medium and also to make sure that faculty learn to employ enough course management technology to teach their course content and communicate interactively with their students electronically.

The distance education office should provide technical support to students so that faculty do not need to do so. Faculty can then spend more time interacting with students, since they don't need to worry about teaching technical skills to students. The instructional designers can also provide course management guidelines for faculty as they teach online. This support helps to mitigate faculty concerns about excessive time related to online courses when compared to face-to-face courses. This is an important factor to faculty and needs to be understood by administration, especially in view of a National Education Association survey finding that faculty members "spend more time on their distance courses than they do on their traditional courses" (Howell, Williams, & Lindsay, 2003, p. 6). Finally, instructional designers need to design courses that are compliant with the World Wide Web Consortium's Web Content Accessibility Guidelines and are "Bobby compliant," that is, accessible by those with visual or hearing impairments.

The Network Support of Distance Education

The backbone of any distance education program is the technology that delivers the online curricula. Very importantly, its technology infrastructure such as servers, network hardware, available Internet bandwidth, and support staff must be scaled to the number of student course enrollments. Adult learners rely on the institution's technology to deliver their distance learning course material on a 24/7 basis. Most adult learners are likely to be online working on their courses' web sites after regular business hours. Retaining students in online courses and degree programs is a matter of providing optimal service. The goal is to maximize the technology so that the course delivery mechanism is seamless, transparent, and dependable, allowing the faculty and students to focus on the e-learning experience.

There are four criteria for network support to ensure that students are able to connect to their courses.

- The distance education staff installing and maintaining this operation must understand that their responsibilities require 24/7 vigilance. Working in the evening and on weekends is likely to be necessary. Rather than crisis management, high-availability planning and system redundancy should be built into the hardware to offset any catastrophic occurrence. The 24/7 expectation also enables staff to perform upgrades and system maintenance during time frames that will least affect students, faculty, and staff.

- This operation requires that the proficiency and knowledge base of the staff remain on the cutting edge. Technology must continually be upgraded, and research must be ongoing to identify the hardware and software that best meet the needs of the recipients. This is expensive—there is no reduction anticipated in the near future, but these costs are essential. These costs must factor in the expenses to deal with virus attacks.

- System redundancy is of utmost importance. Resource monitoring with provisions for automated assumption of services by a secondary fail-over system is imperative. Simply stated, if equipment carrying the course load fails, another server must automatically pick up the load and continue the delivery of the course content.

- The staff in this operation must maintain constant communication with the administrative operation for distance education. This is why many colleges and universities have moved technical support for distance education from their information technology operation to the administrative office for distance education.

As good as the network support may be, students still need to be able to connect to the institution's server from their home. Thus, institutions need to publish the computer requirements for distance education in any printed materials and post the information to their web site. Figure 10.1 provides an example of this from The University of Toledo's web site.

FIGURE 10.1

Computer Requirements at The University of Toledo

Minimum Computer Requirements
CPU: Pentium II 300 MHz, 128MB RAM (Mac equivalent)
Monitor: 800x600, 256 color
Hard Drive: 1.5GB
Removable Media: CD-ROM drive & 3.5" floppy
Sound: Soundcard, speakers or headphones
System: MS Windows 98 or later (or MAC equivalent)
Modem: 56 Kbps
Browser: Internet Explorer 5.0 or later. Must have Internet Service Provider.

Recommended Computer Requirements
CPU: Pentium III 600 MHz, 256MB RAM
Monitor: 1024x768, 256 color
Hard Drive: 20 GB
Removable Media: 32x CD-ROM drive; DVD capability; 3.5" Floppy; Iomega Zip 250
Sound: 8 Bit Soundcard, speakers or headphones
System: MS Windows 2000 SP2, XP SP1 (or MAC equivalent)
Modem: Cable Modem or DSL (150 Kbps)
Browser: Internet Explorer 6.0 or later with appropriate plugins. (See chart for supported browsers.) Must have Internet Service Provider.

In addition, institutions need to indicate that students are responsible for purchasing, installing, and maintaining all computer hardware and software required for their online courses.

When designing online courses, institutions must ensure that students are able to receive and download the coursework from their home computer. Students' Internet Service Providers that provide only 56 Kbps will not be able to successfully access course content that is designed with more than five to ten minutes of video streaming. In fact, the connectivity in students' homes is an element in which we can expect to see change in the near future. In a society that embraces technology, connectivity at 150 Kbps needs to be available to homes in more regions and its cost needs to be affordable to more citizens. The cost of DSL connectivity (150 Kbps) may not be affordable to the vast majority of students wanting to enter higher education via distance education.

Lessons Learned

This section provides tools and insights that can aid administrators at any stage of the distance learning experience. First, working within distance education requires diligence, persistence, dedication, and patience. This is because distance education changes the delivery of higher education from the face-to-face traditional classroom to the virtual classroom. This change is resisted by many and even attacked by a few colleagues. The negative assertions about online teaching and learning may take many forms. But the dialogue is likely to focus on the core of what we strive for in higher education—a quality learning experience. It is important to remember that change is often resisted and that colleagues in higher education are able to cloak their resistance in well-articulated rhetoric that is both argumentative and persuasive. Too, some colleagues feel threatened that distance education will replace the traditional manner of teaching students. Be ready to repeat yourself and to withstand the resistance. It is best to do so by paying attention to the details of the distance education operation, keeping records up to date and in meticulous order, and instilling professionalism and service with team-oriented principles in the distance education staff.

Second, many colleges and institutions have concentrated their efforts on converting courses to an online format without establishing services attuned to their online students. A distance education program that hopes to thrive must be structured to the demands of enrolling students. I refer the reader to the section on student services.

Third, the most successful distance education programs are not built in isolation. It is important to understand the benefit of forming partnerships and collaborations with colleagues and leaders in the academy. Remember that recognition and reliance on the support of colleagues forges effectiveness and results in synergistic efforts. Some of these include:

- Grant proposals can be written to support both the distance education program and an academic area so that equipment and financial support can be sought for the mutual benefit of each operation. Institutions can collaborate on grants to form partnerships, such as a partnership between a community college and four-year university to foster degree completion programs.

- Faculty fellowships can be proposed for the development of online courses and degree programs. The amount of funding can increase as distance education matures within the institution.

- Faculty should be recognized for their support of distance education. This recognition does not always need to be monetary, for example, it can be in the form of a recognition dinner with the awarding of plaques.

- Upper administration should form an advisory forum to provide guidance for the distance education operation. Decisions made and policies adopted by this kind of group build upon the mission and purpose of distance education.

Fourth, it is vital to plan methodically with a strategic plan. This should include a plan and process to deal with a potential failure of the distance education servers and loss of key people on the staff. Even the most carefully planned technical setup can still malfunction. A process to handle each event should be written down and may be, in the beginning, as elementary as listing staff's contact information. Establishing a team effort not only builds a knowledge base among staff members but also strengthens the unit if someone resigns or becomes ill.

Fifth, attend conferences and make presentations. This provides networking with colleagues external to your institution whose work is in distance education. It also imparts the opportunity for benchmarking, revitalizes one's efforts, and enables one to take valuable ideas back to one's home institution. Ideas can be gleaned and formulated for future projects, and new technology can be assessed. Presentations force the unit to define and organize their work and allow for useful discussion with colleagues on specific topics. This is an ideal arena in which to collaborate with faculty involved with distance education.

Finally, remember that while higher education is a slow-moving vehicle, distance education and its technology, while relative newcomers to the academy, are moving with phenomenal speed. This situation is likely to cause distress at times.

Conclusion

Access for adult learners to higher education has increased dramatically due to distance education. Technology increases options for these students in their choice of a college or university program of study. Institutions that structure their distance learning operation with an understanding of the potential students' complex lifestyles will draw not only adult learners but traditional age students. Access to admission, schedule, and registration information from student service professionals is imperative, as well as technical support. This does not remove personnel from the academy or even remove personnel from contact with students. It does require that personnel must understand the needs of the students who enroll in distance education. For example, the student services and tech support personnel for distance education at my university are exceedingly busy communicating with and responding to students on the phone and by email on a daily basis.

Faculty expertise and knowledge are key ingredients for success in distance education. Without the willingness of faculty to reinvent their teaching and rethink their course's learning outcomes, there can be no distance education in the academy. This is because it is not a matter of using technology for teaching and learning but rather a matter of applying the technology to delivering the teaching and learning. Bates's (2000) statement that "students do not so much interact with the technology as through the technology with teachers and other learners" (p. 27) should be remembered. In fact, the quality level of higher education in the online application is maintained by creative online teaching that infuses and builds pathways for critical thinking and its reflective communication. The development of online courses is most effective when a centralized distance education organization provides faculty with comprehensive technical support and training. In this way, faculty as the subject matter experts may concentrate on conversion of the course contact to the online environment. This demands the rigor that faculty bring to the academy and the investment of their time and talent, as the academy responds to the transformation brought by distance education to higher education.

As the academy continues to respond to the growing demand for distance education, the fact that so many traditional age students now mirror the profile of adult students accelerates the pace at which policies and procedures will be adopted that better serve the adult learner. At many universities and colleges, enrollment of traditional age students far outnumbers enrollment of adult students in distance education courses and degree programs. In fact, distance education originally was organized to increase enrollment from outside the designated commuter region of some universities or colleges. As such, it was considered a marginal operation for adult students or those unable to commute to the campuses' traditional classrooms and its reporting line was to a division of the college or university designated for nontraditional learners.

Many in the academy were at first perplexed by the ever-increasing number of enrolling traditional age students living within commuting distance of the campuses and even in their own dorms. This changing pattern of enrollment "has forced a rethinking of institutional strategies even among traditional universities" (Hanna, 2003, p. 68). Many institutions are responding by moving the reporting line of distance education to the college or university's academic affairs office. This has resulted in greater access to higher education for adult students as society catapults into the twenty-first century, an age in which communication via cyberspace is considered commonplace.

The availability of courses and complete degree programs via distance education will continue to impact the process of lifelong learning that is so necessary for our fast-paced society. This will allow students to pursue their educational goals and be able to better balance all the responsibilities of their lives. Though a range of involvement in distance education exists in the academy, it seems clear that more learning opportunities at more colleges and universities will be available via technology in the future. This can mean that society will experience significant changes, such as increases in college graduation rates, because citizens who could not begin a college degree or return to the traditional college classroom will be able to do so in the virtual college classroom.

References

Allen, I. E., & Seaman, J. (2003, September). *Sizing the opportunity: The quality and extent of online education in the United States, 2002 and 2003.* Needham, MA: Sloan-C. Retrieved September 23, 2004, from http://www.sloan-c.org/resources/sizing_opportunity.pdf

Bash, L. (2003). *Adult learners in the academy.* Bolton, MA: Anker.

Bates, A. W. (2000). *Managing technological change: Strategies for college and university leaders.* San Francisco, CA: Jossey-Bass.

Beaudoin, M. F. (2003, Summer). Distance education leadership for the new century. *Online Journal of Distance Learning Administration, 6*(2). Retrieved September 23, 2004, from http://www.westga.edu/~distance/ojdla/summer62/beaudoin62.html

Cureton, J. (2003). *Wired and tired: Portrait of today's college students.* Paper presented at the fifth annual WebCT User Conference, San Diego, CA.

Diaz, D. P. (2002, May/June). Online drop rates revisited. *The Technology Source.* Retrieved March 20, 2004, from http://ts.mivu.org/default.asp?show=article&id=981

Giegerich, S. (2003, July 18). Survey finds enrollment in long-distance program has more than doubled. *CBS News.com.* Retrieved September 23, 2004, from http://www.cbsnews.com/stories/2003/07/18/tech/main563947.shtml?CMP=ILC-SearchStories

Gould, E. (2003). *Accreditation issues in online learning.* Paper presented at the Ohio Learning Network Conference, Columbus, OH.

Hanna, D. E. (2003). Organizational models in higher education, past and future. In M. G. Moore & W. G. Anderson (Eds.), *Handbook of distance education* (pp. 67–79). Mahwah, NJ: Lawrence Erlbaum.

(2003, September). Helping students become tech-savvy will aid in retention. *Nontraditional Students Report, 5*(12), 3.

Higher Learning Commission of the North Central Association of Colleges and Schools. (2002). *Best practices for electronically offered degrees and certificate programs.* Chicago, IL: Author. Retrieved September 24, 2004, from http://www.ncahigherlearningcommission.org/resources/electronic_degrees/Best_Pract_DEd.pdf

Howell, S. L., Williams, P. B., & Lindsay, N. K. (2003, Fall). Thirty-two trends affecting distance education: An informed foundation for strategic planning. *Online Journal of Distance Learning Administration, 6*(3), 1–19.

Johnstone, S. M., Ewell, P., & Paulson, K. (2002). *Student learning as academic currency.* Washington, DC: American Council on Education.

Lorenzetti, J. P. (2002). Before they drift away: Two experts pool retention insights. *Distance Education Report, 6*(8), 1–2.

Oblinger, D. (2003, July/August). Boomers, gen-xers, & millennials: Understanding the new students. *EDUCAUSE Review,* 37–47. Retrieved September 24, 2004, from http://www.educause.edu/ir/library/pdf/erm0342.pdf

Scollin, P. A., & Tello, S. F. (1999). Implementing distance learning: Frameworks for change. *The Internet and Higher Education, 2*(1), 11–20.

U.S. Department of Education, National Center for Education Statistics. (2002). *The condition of education 2002* (NCES 2002–025). Washington, DC: U.S. Government Printing Office. Retrieved September 21, 2004, from http://www.inpathways.net/high%20school%20academic%20preparation.pdf

Verduin, J. R., & Clark, T. A. (1991). *Distance education: The foundations of effective practice.* San Francisco, CA: Jossey-Bass.

Weigel, V. B. (2002). *Deep learning for a digital age: Technology's untapped potential to enrich higher education.* San Francisco, CA: Jossey-Bass.

Winters, R. (2000, September 18). Going back to class online. *Time, 156*(12), G8–G11.

11

Computer-Mediated Communication: A Quest for Quality

Margie Martyn

Computer-mediated communication (CMC) in its simplest form is the process of exchanging thoughts, ideas, and information via a computer keyboard and screen connected to other computers (Lewis, Whitaker, & Julian, 1995). This definition covers the nuts and bolts of CMC, but it only scratches the surface of the potential for interaction and communication that can be achieved by computer. The underlying message is that this type of communication has a benefit to faculty and students who utilize it, especially for adult learners who are juggling multiple responsibilities and roles. With exposure to CMC increasing in the workplace and in daily life, it is not surprising that working adults find value in the computer-mediated learning environment (Van Rooij, 2000). According to Gault, Herring, Morris, and Szydlo (2002), "Time plus energy equals learning. Learning to use one's time well is critical for students and professionals alike. Allocating realistic amounts of time means effective learning for students and effective teaching for faculty" (p. 13).

This chapter articulates how CMC can develop community, provide quality interactions, distill knowledge, provide a social presence, lower transactional distance, and be an equalizer between racial, ethnic, and gender groups. Choosing the appropriate tool to accomplish the specific task is essential if CMC is to be used effectively. This challenge is stated best by Lewis, Whitaker, and Julian (1995):

As distance education increasingly uses the array of new tools becoming available, some will open up new opportunities for learning and human development. New challenges will also arise that were not dreamt of in the early stages. CMC will have a big part in these developments, both as a solution and as an originator of challenges. (p. 23)

Determining Quality

Both researchers and organizations have focused on interaction as the primary criteria to address when assessing quality. Garrison (1993) points out that "quality is reflected in the nature and frequency of communication between teacher and student as well as between student and student" (p. 11).

The Ohio Learning Network (OLN) is the state of Ohio's e-learning consortium representing public and private institutions of higher education. OLN is an advocate for effective practices and policies that support e-learning. In 2002, a task force convened by OLN determined that quality is defined in many ways, but the basic elements involve the interaction among and between faculty and students (Ohio Learning Network, 2002). The purpose of the report was to establish guidelines for determining the quality in online courses. The report used Chickering and Gamson's (1987) Seven Principles for Good Practice in Undergraduate Education as the foundation. Quality is measured by looking at the following seven principles:

1) Encourage interaction between learner and instructor.

2) Encourage collaboration among students.

3) Encourage active learning.

4) Encourage time on task.

5) Encourage prompt feedback.

6) Encourage the setting of high expectations of learning.

7) Encourage the appreciation of diversity in learning methods and style.

According to a recent report, electronic technologies are being used to improve quality in many ways, for example, "using technology in ways that enhance faculty-student interaction or that attract students to spend more time on task" (Higher Learning Commission, 2002, p. 6). The focus on interaction is echoed in principles, guidelines, and benchmarks of many respected authorities including the American Council on Education and The Alliance, National Education Association, Council for Higher Education Accreditation, and University Continuing Education Association (Martyn & Bash, 2002). Computer-mediated communication provides a venue for adult students to interact more with both faculty and other students, as well as spend more time on task. In the past, these interactions were achieved solely in the class sessions in which adult learners came to campus.

Having established the need for interaction in distance learning courses to ensure quality, this chapter will evaluate the research on interaction and its impact on satisfaction and learning outcomes for adult learners. Based on the research, best practices will be outlined for implementing and integrating interaction into distance learning courses.

Interaction Types

Moore (1989) identified three major types of interaction found in most learning environments: learner-content, learner-instructor, and learner-learner. Recent research illuminates the value of the three types of interaction.

Learner-Content

According to Moore and Kearsley (1996), learner-content interaction is the very foundation of learning and is required in any learning transaction. The learner must have the opportunity to interact with new concepts, principles, and theories. Taking a constructivist bent, the learner must assimilate the new information into his or her cognitive structures and define new meanings and knowledge. CMC can be utilized to accomplish this type of interaction through course content modules, external web resource links, electronic simulations and cases, and through electronic PowerPoint presentations and other course modules. According to King (1998), these skills are especially important for adult learners: "Adult learners need to refine their analysis and evaluation skills as they traverse the world of the Web" (p. 26). Adult learners who did not experience computers at a young age may experience some stress when dealing with this type of content-student interaction (Eastmond, 1998).

Instructor-Learner

The goals of instructor-learner interaction are to stimulate student interest, facilitate learning, and to organize evaluation and provide feedback (Moore, 1989). According to Moore and Kearsley (1996), this type of interaction is thought to be necessary by most faculty members and essential by most learners. Although some distance learning courses provide independent learning, students value the interaction with faculty in online courses (Jiang, 1998; Jiang & Ting, 1999). Faculty members can provide the correct pacing, guidance, mentoring, and encouragement, and determine if there are problems or misconceptions.

Anderson and Garrison (1998) reported that "learner-teacher communication goes to the heart of education—both face-to-face and at a distance" (p. 101). They also indicated that

> Interaction between learner and teacher is essential to assess current understanding, design appropriate approaches (e.g., depth, pacing) stimulate critical reflection, and diagnose misconception. These elements of support are required whether educational communication is mediated technologically or occurs in a conventional face-to-face environment. (p. 102)

Through this type of interaction, the instructor can provide a "means of assistance" as described by Savery (2003). This categorization is delineated by Gallimore and Tharp (1990) and identifies different types of interactions including feeding back, instructing, questioning, cognitive structuring, modeling, and contingency management. Instructor-learner interaction also provides support for the novice learners through scaffolding. "Scaffolding involves supporting novice learners by limiting the complexities of the learning context and gradually removing those limits" (Dabbagh, 2003, p. 40). According to Dabbagh, scaffolding is expedited through the use of web-based course management tools. These tools are especially convenient to adult learners who usually have access to the Internet from home and the workplace.

Research on the results of learner-instructor interaction is vast. Many studies found that students experienced a greater level of satisfaction in distance learning courses when they engaged in meaningful and frequent interaction with the instructor (DeBourgh, 1998; Drnek, 1998; Jiang & Ting, 1999; Mowen & Parks, 1997). Geary (1998) found that students placed more value on instructor-learner interaction in a distance learning course than they do in face-to-face courses. According to Geary, it seemed that students had learned not to expect interaction in traditional courses but found it important in distance learning courses. Learner satisfaction does make a difference. Mowen and Parks (1997) found learner satisfaction to be a significant factor affecting a learner's persistence in distance learning courses. Baker (2001) went a step further and tried to discover how the instructor-learner interaction affected student learning outcomes. He found that instructor immediacy (which means that students feel the instructor is a "real person" and that they feel a social closeness to the instructor) was the singular predictor of effective learning. Gilbert (2002) indicated similar findings, stating that many of the new media options offer ways of personalizing communication between students and faculty, enabling all involved to connect more fully as human beings, not just those who deliver and receive sterile information. Social presence can be increased by using emoticons [*e.g.*, :) or ;)], using more first- person language, sharing personal information with students, and responding quickly to email and discussion posts.

Another concept is based on the transactional distance theory. This theory states that a student may feel that distance in online courses is based more on pedagogy than actual geography. According to this theory, transactional distance is a function of structure (if the course is lecture, which is high structure) and dialogue (interaction). A lower transactional distance will occur when there is less structure and more dialogue. In a study by Rossman (1999) that compared 221 graduate nursing students in two formats, there was actually lower transactional distance in the online course than in the face-to-face course. Saba and Shearer (1994) used an experimental study to show the correlation between the structure and dialogue. Online courses have the opportunity to reduce transactional distance because there is usually less structure—less lecturing and more discussion. Adult students appreciate this opportunity for dialogue. As self-directed learners, adult students want the opportunity to ask questions and shape their own learning. According to Brookfield (1986), "The exercise of autonomous self-directed learning is proposed as the distinguishing characteristic of adult learning" (p. 26).

Learner-Learner

Bates (1990) found that interaction between the learner and other learners is possibly the most important interaction for many learners, but it has tended to be neglected in distance education. According to Moore and Kearsley (1996), this is a relatively new development in online learning. Because of the software available, there are more opportunities for learners to interact with each other. Garrison (1993) found that students play a very important role in facilitating the cognitive development of fellow-learners.

In a study by Webster and Hackley (1997), the researchers found that learning is best accomplished through the active involvement of students. Bischoff, Bisconer, Kooker, and Woods (1996) found that many students actually seek online group learning environments because they enjoy collaboration with other students. Other research findings support the value of student-student interaction (Edens, 2000; Serwatka, 2002). Many researchers found that CMC expedited the communication between diverse types of students. CMC leveled the playing field and removed barriers due to physical disabilities, gender, ethnicity, learning style, or personality type, as confirmed by Funaro and Montelle (1999), Gillette (2001), and Graham, Scarbourough, and Goodwin (1999).

According to Berge (1995), there is an emerging body of literature from faculty who speak from their own experiences concerning the empowerment of persons with disabilities, physical impairment, disfigurement, or speech impediments which hinder their equal participation in face-to-face encounters. CMC promotes an equalization of users since it is, at present, primarily text-only. The consequent reduction in social cues leads to a protective ignorance surrounding a person's social role and status.

Integrating CMC Into the Curriculum

Understanding the value of interaction is important, but how can it be integrated into the curriculum? What does the literature on CMC suggest as the most effective uses for each of the tools as they relate to the different types of interaction?

Time Format Consideration

Computer-managed course management software such as Blackboard or WebCT provides a range of CMC tools to support these three types of interactions. The first variable to consider when investigating these tools is based on time. CMC tools can be either synchronous (same time) or asynchronous (any time). An example of a synchronous CMC tool would be chat. The chat tool works when the instructor and students log on to the computer at the same time and communicate with one another simultaneously. This constructive, interactive exchange of ideas has been dubbed "the missing link in online instruction" because the instructor engages students through posing thought-provoking questions (Roberson & Klotz, 2001). Examples of asynchronous CMC would include announcements, digital drop box, electronic Blackboard note area, email, group tools, online content modules, online surveys, online technical manuals, online threaded discussion, online quizzes, and student web pages.

Synchronous communications are best used when the information or learning being conveyed is time sensitive, immediacy of feedback is important, and all participants are available to meet simultaneously (Shea-Schultz & Fogarty, 2002). Conversely, asynchronous methods provide the optimum benefit when deeper reflection or learning is required, real-time interaction does not provide particular value, and the flexibility of anytime/anywhere is desired (Shea-Schultz & Fogarty, 2002).

Effective Uses

There is a plethora of literature on best practices in utilizing each of the CMC tools available. Berge and Muilenburg (2002) describe the best way to ask questions in a discussion board designed for adult learning. One of the suggestions for promoting discussion with adults is to provide a venue for discussing adult life experiences and allowing students to pose questions to fellow learners. Berge and Muilenburg propose the use of Bloom's (1956) taxonomy as a base for asking questions at each level.

- Recall

- Comprehension

- Application

- Analysis

- Synthesis

- Evaluation

They state that by utilizing Bloom's taxonomy, instructors can be careful to generate questions that will require a higher level of thinking and develop students who are critical thinkers.

Klemm (2000) provides some excellent practical suggestions for utilizing discussion threads. He indicates that students must be trained on how to submit quality posts, which are based on research and documentation—not opinion. He also states that students must be taught the proper netiquette (web etiquette) and learn to respect the opinions of others. He feels that posts must be graded in order to ensure that students participate fully.

Knowlton, Knowlton, and Davis (2000) also have suggestions for providing quality discussion posts. They articulate the need to require that students provide a deliverable or project that is due out of the process. They also believe that instructors need to model appropriate discussion thread behavior. Adult students appreciate this concrete feedback and clear direction (Willis, 2002).

Brown (2003) has valuable suggestions for other CMC uses. He believes that the instructor can create a sense of community before the class even starts by sending a welcome message to the whole class via email. The faculty member can also use the instructor page to include some personal information about himself or herself (e.g., hobbies like bike riding) so that the student can develop a stronger social presence with the instructor. To clarify content during the course, Brown states that the instructor could have students email a "muddy" point, or the faculty member could develop a FAQ (frequently asked question) document and post it in the course content section. Then students could have many answers available at once. This is also an efficiency measure for the instructor who often gets the same questions term after term.

Dabbagh (2003) states that with the changes in the course management systems like Blackboard, WebCT and eCollege, faculty have the potential to use CMC tools even more because of the ease of use of the tools and the ability of the tools to interact with students.

Components of CMC

Based on the research, each of the components of CMC provides particular value to student learning outcomes and satisfaction as outlined below. The components are divided into three sections: communication tools, content tools, and organizational and management tools.

Communication Tools

Chat. This synchronous tool provides a method for instructors and students to meet at the same time. The students and instructor communicate at the same time in a virtual classroom. In the virtual classroom, which is simply a web page with communication tools and links, students and faculty can send text messages, look at a White Board, and search the World Wide Web. Students can raise their virtual hands when they have a question, or even send a private question to the instructor. This tool can also be used for virtual office hours to facilitate interaction and learning on a one-to-one basis. Online group chats can be effective learning methods in which the exchange of ideas between instructor and students occurs as a group. Roberson and Klotz (2001) dub it "the missing link" in online instruction. They state that chat can provide structure and continuous interaction with faculty. Irvine (2000) found that a much larger portion of the class participated in a chat situation than face-to-face. Kimbrough (1999) found a correlation between frequency of participation in online chats and course performance. Martyn (2003) found that participation in the online chat helped students to stay current and improved retention in an online course. Chats have the ability to be archived and referenced at a later time. Hammer (2002) found a correlation between students' participation in chat and scores on the final exam. Female students seem to particularly like participating in chat and participated more often, according to Davidson-Shivers, Muilenburg, and Tanner (2001).

Email. Email is one of the most frequently used CMC tools (Teles, 2002). Email is the transmission of messages over communication networks. The messages can be entered through a keyboard, electronic files stored on a disk, or downloaded from a personal digital assistant device (PDA). One of the biggest advantages of using email is that most learners and instructors are familiar with its use and are comfortable using it. The amount of learning can be high in email discussions (Owen, Pollard, Kilpatrick, & Rumley, 1998). Savery (2003) found that email provided students and instructors an opportunity to interact at a distance on a common topic and provided a variety of ways for faculty to assist students. Email provides one-on-one mentoring and guidance for an individual student (Dabbagh, 2003), or can be sent to a group of students. Email messages can also be archived and reused after customization for another student.

Leh (2001) conducted a study that looked at how email had developed a sense of social presence and community. The study showed that email interaction between the instructor and students increased the social presence. Leh did a follow-up survey a year later that confirmed the results.

Group tools. Many course management systems have a special section for student groups to work. The group tools mirror the other CMC tools that are used in the course and usually include a chat, online threaded discussion, and digital drop box area. The group tools are housed in a separate area and can be accessed only by the students in a particular group. Here the team can work independently of the rest of the class and collaborate on projects. According to Alexander (1995), students construct and interpret the meaning from a range of people, and then construct their own individual meaning. Having the students explore and utilize the group tools prepares them for future endeavors in business, industry, and the nonprofit sector. Students have access to a wider range of perspectives via the Internet than they ever had in a face-to-face class. This diversity in perspective offers an unprecedented environment for experimentation in collaborative learning, going beyond normal teacher-student interactions in a face-to-face class to synergistic explorations with diverse groups (Holt, Kleiber, Swenson, Rees, & Milton, 1998; Schrire, 2002).

Online threaded discussion. Online threaded discussion provides a way to analyze and synthesize course content and construct new meaning. The online threaded discussion consists of a web page on which a faculty member can post a thought-provoking question, and on which students can reply to the question and post a response. The replies are considered threads because as students reply to both the original question and to the responses of other students, the discussion begins to weave into a variety of topics and areas. Students are more willing to participate due to a measure of anonymity. It motivates students when they feel empowered to express their own ideas (Kubala, 1998).

According to Goldberg (2000), there are as many ways to use group electronic discussions as there are ways to teach. They are very powerful tools, and a part of that power comes from the versatility with which they can be applied. "Students can make connections and build relationships with their classmates through discussion. More importantly than helping students feel connected, online discussions have distinct educational benefits. Through discussion students can gain a broader perspective of course material" (Knowlton, Knowlton, & Davis, 2000, p. 54). Theodore (2001) found that online discussions enhanced teaching and learning by involving students personally, and that they facilitated a more complete presentation of course content and aided in the development of thinking skills.

Student home pages. Learners can introduce themselves to one another through the student home page section of a course management system, establishing an atmosphere of trust and community. The student home page is a structured page where the student can post an opening message, some personal information that he or she wishes to share, a picture, and some web links to favorite music, movies, or hobbies. The students can also describe their employment status, educational goals, and life experiences. This tool has the potential to increase social presence, or the degree to which a person is perceived as "real" in mediated communication (Gunawardena & Zittle, 1997). Social presence is a strong predictor of overall satisfaction in a text-based distance learning course (Gunawardena & Zittle, 1997).

Content Tools

Announcement page. The announcement page is a web page that students first access when entering a course. This communication tool provides students with an asynchronous venue that can be accessed any time the students wants to view course updates. This ability to post information efficiently to all students has been shown to have benefits to faculty who teach online (Branon & Essex, 2001; Teles, 2002). Dabbagh (2003) states that the announcement page can help students stay current with course projects and due dates, as well as provide encouragement and social presence.

External links. External links are web links listed on a separate web page in the course management system. The web links provide a link to extra material on the World Wide Web or in electronic databases. King (1998) found that the development and improvement of dynamic resources is a simple but empowering tool for adult learners to refine their analysis and evaluation skills. The plethora of information available on the Internet can provide updated and more current information for learners. The use of web link features can present questions for critical thinking (Dabbagh, 2003).

Online content modules. Online course content including lecture notes, PowerPoint slides, and electronic case studies provides students with 24/7 access to course materials.

Organizational and Management Tools

Digital drop box and online grade book. The digital drop box is an extremely beneficial tool for students to get feedback. It consists of a web page that has clear instructions for a student to send a file to the instructor via a browse button. The instructor can then download the file, add comments, and upload the file back into the student's digital drop box. It is an organized and efficient way for faculty to manage their grading process. Chism (n.d.) notes the benefit of quick feedback for students and points out that it often alleviates the need to "unlearn" misconceptions. The drop box is more efficient than email because it keeps the document in a location that won't be lost.

Electronic blackboard note area. This tool is a web page that provides a place for students to write course notes or keep an online reflective journal. Only the student has access to this area. The student types in the notes and can retrieve and print them later. The emphasis on the written word encourages a deeper level of thinking in online classes (Smith, Ferguson, & Caris, 2001).

Online surveys. Online surveys provide instructors with the opportunity to get feedback on how the students perceive the course is progressing. Questions about teaching style, projects, and learning activities can be generated in a short time. Students have the opportunity to respond anonymously. The potential for formative evaluation allows the instructor to fine-tune the course at any time during the term.

Online technical manual. Sherry (2000) articulates the importance of providing a means for students to receive technical help. The research shows that student familiarity and confidence with the software will lead to student satisfaction and improved learning outcomes (DeBourgh, 1999).

Online quizzes. Online quizzes provide students with the opportunity to interact with the content and to receive immediate feedback on areas that need more study. Immediate feedback is more effective than feedback delivered after a delay (Dempsey, Driscoll, & Swindell, 1993). A correlational study that investigated diverse variables in the online environment found there was a significant positive relationship between instructor feedback and student satisfaction among the learners. In a study by Coates and Humphreys (2001), the statistical analysis showed that online quizzes positively correlated with student performance on exams, while passive reading of course content did not. The researchers hypothesized that the active engagement with course content was of primary importance.

"Web-based course management tools are now making it easier for teachers to assume supportive and facilitative roles due to their comprehensive and integrative nature, user-friendliness, and embedded user support systems" (Dabbagh, 2003, p. 43). Many of the new media options offer ways of personalizing communication between students and faculty, enabling all involved to connect more fully as human beings, not just as those who deliver and receive sterile information (Gilbert, 2002).

CMC Benchmarks and Lessons Learned

Based on the research described above, faculty should adhere to the following guidelines when integrating CMC into their courses.

- Relate the use of CMC to course objectives.

- Empower the learners to participate in course direction and learning outcomes through CMC.

- Utilize open-ended questions to encourage more diverse responses and critical thinking.

- Pose questions and scenarios that require learners to utilize their own experience.

- Teach students the process of using CMC as well as course content.

- Model effective CMC techniques for students.

- Require participation so that all students participate and receive benefits.

- Form learning teams to promote collaborative learning.

- Provide feedback within 24 to 48 hours on postings and emails.

- Utilize student moderators in the online threaded discussion.

- Participate and facilitate but do not dominate.

- Provide the proper scaffolding and support as students engage in complex processes outside their comfort zone.

Conclusion

Computer-mediated communication has the potential to increase quality interactions between students, students and course content, and students and instructors. These interactions will improve the quality learning outcomes of students as reflected in Chickering and Gamson (1987). CMC is especially effective for adult students who may not be as comfortable with the new technology, but realize that it is becoming increasingly important in their everyday lives.

> No one can deny that we have entered an information age in which power comes to those who have information and know how to access it. If we consider what factors of CMC will be most important to education in the information age, it seems that our goals should be to develop self-motivated learners and help people learn to find and share information. If designed well, CMC applications can be used effectively to facilitate collaboration among students as peers, teachers as learners and facilitators, and guests or experts from outside the classroom. (Berge, 1995, p. 22)

See Appendix 11A for a synthesis of the various modes of CMC and the corresponding learning outcomes.

References

Alexander, S. (1995). *Teaching and learning on the World Wide Web.* Lismore, Australia: Southern Cross University. Retrieved September 29, 2004, from http://ausweb.scu.edu.au/aw95/education2/alexander/

Allen, M., Bourhis, J., Burrell, N., & Mabry, E. (2002). Comparing student satisfaction with distance education to traditional classrooms in higher education: A meta-analysis. *American Journal of Distance Education, 16*(2), 83–97.

Anderson, T. D., & Garrison, D. R. (1998). Learning in a networked world: New roles and responsibilities. In C. C. Gibson (Ed.), *Distance learners in higher education: Institutional responses for quality outcomes* (pp. 97–112). Madison, WI: Atwood.

Bailey, Y. S., & Wright, V. H. (2000). *Innovative uses of threaded discussion groups.* Paper presented at the annual meeting of the Mid-South Educational Research Association, Bowling Green, KY. (ERIC Document Reproduction Service No. ED446 716)

Baker, J. (2001). The effects of instructor immediacy and student cohesiveness on affective and cognitive learning in the online classroom (Doctoral dissertation, Regent University, 2001). *Dissertation Abstracts International, 62,* 2081.

Bates, A. (1990). *Interactivity as a criterion for media selection in distance education.* Paper presented at the annual conference of the Asian Association of Open Universities, Jakarta, Indonesia.

Berge, Z. (1995). Facilitating computer conferencing: Recommendations from the field. *Educational Technology, 35*(1), 22–30.

Berge, Z., & Muilenburg, L. (2000, September/October). Designing discussion questions for online adult learning. *Educational Technology, 40*(5), 53–56.

Bischoff, W. R., Bisconer, S. W., Kooker, B. M., & Woods, L. C. (1996). Transactional distance and interactive television in the distance education of health professionals. *American Journal of Distance Education, 10*(3), 4–19.

Bloom, B. S. (Ed.). (1956). *Taxonomy of educational objectives: The classification of educational goals: Handbook I, cognitive domain.* New York, NY: Longmans, Green.

Branon, R. F., & Essex, C. (2001). Synchronous and asynchronous communication tools in distance education: A survey of instructors. *TechTrends, 45*(1), 36, 42.

Brookfield, S. D. (1986). *Understanding and facilitating adult learning.* San Francisco, CA: Jossey-Bass.

Brown, D. (2003, May). Encouraging good student contact. *Syllabus, 16*(13). Retrieved September 29, 2004, from http://www.syllabus.com/article.asp?id=7630

Cheng, H., Lehman, J., & Armstrong, P. (1991). Comparison of performance and attitude in traditional and computer conferencing classes. *American Journal of Distance Education, 5*(3), 51–64.

Chickering, A. W., & Gamson, Z. F. (1987, March). Seven principles for good practice in undergraduate education. *AAHE Bulletin, 39*(7), 3–7.

Chism, N. (n.d.). *Handbook for instructors on the use of electronic class discussion.* Columbus, OH: Ohio State University, Office of Faculty and TA Development. Retrieved September 29, 2004, from http://ftad.osu.edu/Publications/elecdisc/pages/index.htm

Coates, D., & Humphreys, B. R. (2001). Evaluation of computer-assisted instruction in principles of economics. *Educational Technology and Society, 4*(2), 133–144.

Dabbagh, N. (2003). Scaffolding: An important teacher competency in online learning. *TechTrends for Leaders in Education and Training, 47*(2), 39–44.

Davidson-Shivers, G., Muilenburg, L., & Tanner, E. (2001). How do students participate in synchronous and asynchronous online discussions? *Journal of Educational Computing Research, 25*(4), 351–366.

DeBourgh, G. (1998). Learning and instructional predictors of student satisfaction in a graduate nursing program taught via interactive video teleconferencing and World Wide Web/Internet (Doctoral dissertation, University of San Francisco, 1998). *Dissertation Abstracts International, 59,* 1046.

DeBourgh, G. A. (1999). Technology is the tool, teaching is the task: Student satisfaction in distance learning. *Society for Information Technology and Teacher Education International Conference, 1999*(1), 131–137.

Dempsey, J., Driscoll, M., & Swindell, L. (1993). Text-based feedback. In J. Dempsey & G. Sales (Eds.), *Interactive instruction and feedback* (pp. 21–54). Englewood Cliffs, NJ: Educational Technology Publications.

Drnek, J. M. (1998). Student learning style, satisfaction, perceptions, emotions, and Internet use at a large southwestern university (Doctoral dissertation, Northern Arizona University, 1998). *Dissertation Abstractions International, 59,* 671.

Eastmond, D. V. (1998). Adult learners and Internet-based distance education. In B. Cahoon (Ed.), *New directions for adult and continuing education, No. 78. Adult learning and the Internet* (pp. 33–41). San Francisco, CA: Jossey-Bass.

Edens, K. M. (2000). Promoting communication, inquiry, and reflection in an early practicum experience via an on-line discussion group. *Action in Teacher Education, 22*(2), 14–23.

Funaro, G. M., & Montell, F. (1999). Pedagogical roles and implementation guidelines for online communication tools. *ALN Magazine, 3*(2), 8–15.

Gallimore, R., & Tharp, R. (1990). Teaching mind in society: Teaching, schooling, and literate discourse. In L. C. Moll (Ed.), *Vygotsky and education: Instructional implications and applications of sociohistorical psychology* (pp. 175–205). New York, NY: Cambridge University Press.

Garrison, D. R. (1993). Quality and access in distance education: Theoretical considerations. In D. Keegan (Ed.), *Theoretical principles of distance education* (pp. 9–21). London, England: Rutledge.

Gault, A., Herring, L., Morris, N., & Szydlo, S. (2002). *Seven principles of good practice: A FEEDS evaluation.* Retrieved September 29, 2004, from http://www.unf.edu/dept/cirt/teaching/7principles.pdf

Geary, D. (1998). Perceptions of instructor-student interaction as a reason for persistence in two-way audio & visual distance education (Doctoral dissertation, Virginia Commonwealth University, 1998). *Dissertation Abstracts International, 59,* 2299.

Gilbert, S. W. (2002, June). Making educational technology translucent. *Syllabus, 15*(11). Retrieved September 29, 2004, from http://www.syllabus.com/article.asp?id=6400

Gillette, D. (2001). Extending traditional classroom boundaries. *American Economist, 45*(2), 57–69.

Goldberg, M. (2000). The asynchronous spectrum. *Online Teaching and Learning Newsletter.* Retrieved September 29, 2004, from http://eva.webct.com/service/ViewContent?contentID=2339758

Graham, M., Scarborough, H., & Goodwin, C. (1999). Implementing computer mediated communication in an undergraduate course: A practical experience. *Journal of Asynchronous Learning Networks, 3*(1), 14–28.

Gunawardena, N., & Zittle, F. J. (1997). Social presence as a predictor of satisfaction within a computer-mediated conferencing environment. *American Journal of Distance Education, 11*(3), 8–26.

Hammer, V. A. (2002). The influence of interaction on active learning, learning outcomes, and community building in an online technology course (Doctoral dissertation, University of Cincinnati, 2002). *Dissertation Abstracts International, 63,* 851.

Higher Learning Commission of the North Central Association. (2002). *NCA study team report: The impact of technology in learning and teaching.* Chicago, IL: Author.

Holt, M. E., Kleiber, P. B., Swenson, J. D., Rees, E. R., Milton, J. (1998). Facilitating group learning on the Internet. In B. Cahoon (Ed.), *New directions for adult and continuing education, No. 78. Adult learning and the Internet* (pp. 43–52). San Francisco, CA: Jossey-Bass.

Irvine, S. (2000). *What are we talking about? The impact of computer-mediated communication on student learning.* Paper presented at the Society for Information Technology and Teacher Education International Conference, San Diego, CA. (ERIC Document Reproduction Service No. ED444494)

Jiang, M. (1998). Distance learning in a web-based environment: An analysis of factors influencing students' perceptions of online learning (Doctoral dissertation, State University of New York at Albany, 1998). *Dissertation Abstracts International, 59,* 4044.

Jiang, M., & Ting, E. (1999). *A study of students' perceived learning in a web-based online environment.* Paper presented at the WebNet 99 World Conference on the WWW and Internet, Honolulu, HI. Retrieved September 29, 2004, from http://www2.sjsu.edu/depts/it/edit221/correl1.pdf

Kimbrough, D. R. (1999). Online "chat room" tutorials—an unusual gender bias in computer use. *Journal of Science Education and Technology, 8*(3), 227–234.

King, K. (1998). Course development on the World Wide Web. In B. Cahoon (Ed.), *New directions for adult and continuing education, No. 78. Adult learning and the Internet* (pp. 25–32). San Francisco, CA: Jossey-Bass.

Klemm, W. R. (2000). What's wrong with on-line discussions—and how to fix it. *World Conference on the WWW and Internet, 2000*(1), 335–340.

Knowlton, D. S., Knowlton, H. M., & Davis, C. (2000, June). The whys and hows of online discussion. *Syllabus, 13*(10), 54–58.

Kubala, T. (March, 1998). Addressing student needs: Teaching on the Internet. *T.H.E. Journal, 25*(8), 71–74.

Leh, A. (2001). Computer-mediated communication and social presence in a distance learning environment. *International Journal of Educational Telecommunications, 7*(2), 109–128.

Lewis, J., Whitaker, J., & Julian, J. (1995). Distance education for the 21st century: The future of national and international telecommuting networks in distance education. In Z. L. Berge & M. P. Collins (Eds.), *Computer-mediated communication and the online classroom Vol. III: Distance learning* (pp. 13–30). Cresskill, NJ: Hampton Press.

Martyn, M. (2003). The hybrid online model: Good practice. *Educause Quarterly, 26*(1), 18–23.

Martyn, M., & Bash, L. (2002). *Hybrid distance learning format—a great fit for the small liberal arts college.* Paper presented at the 22nd annual AHEA/ACE Conference, Pittsburgh, PA.

Moore, M. (1989). Distance education, a learner's system. *Lifelong Learning, 12*(8), 8–11.

Moore, M. (2002). What does research say about learners using computer-mediated communication in distance learning? *American Journal of Distance Education, 16*(2), 61–64.

Moore, M., & Kearsley, G. (1996). *Distance education: A systems view.* Belmont, CA: Wadsworth.

Mowen, A., & Parks, S. (1997). Competitive marketing of distance education: A model for placing quality within a strategic planning context. *American Journal of Distance Education, 11*(3), 27–49.

Ohio Learning Network. (2002). *Quality learning in Ohio and at a distance: A report of the Ohio Learning Network task force on quality in distance learning.* Columbus, OH: Author. Retrieved September 29, 2004, from http://www.oln.org/about_oln/pdf/Quality_TF.pdf

Owen, C., Pollard, J., Kilpatrick, S., & Rumley, D. (1998). *Electronic learning communities? Factors that enhance and inhibit learning within email discussion groups.* Paper presented at the International Symposium on Learning Communities, Launceston, Tasmania. (ERIC Document Reproduction Service No. ED451972)

Peters, K. M. (2000). Creative use of threaded discussion areas. *Online Teaching and Learning Newsletter.* Retrieved September 29, 2004, from http://www.webct.com/OTL/ViewContent?contentID=898084

Prammanee, N. (2003). Understanding participation in online courses: A case study of perceptions of online interaction. *Instructional Technology Forum.* Retrieved September 29, 2004, from http://it.coe.uga.edu/itforum/paper68/paper68.html

Roberson, T., & Klotz, J. (2001). *Chat: The missing link in online instruction.* Paper presented at the Mid-South Educational Research Association Conference, Little Rock, AR.

Rossman, M. H. (1999). Successful online teaching using an asynchronous learner discussion forum. *Journal of Asynchronous Learning Networks, 3*(2). Retrieved November 4, 2004, from http://www.sloan-c.org/publications/jaln/v3n2/pdf/v3n2_rossman.pdf

Rovai, A. (2002). Sense of community, perceived cognitive learning, and persistence in asynchronous learning networks. *Internet and Higher Education, 5*(4), 319–332.

Saba, F., & Shearer, R. L. (1994). Verifying key theoretical concepts in a dynamic model of distance education. *American Journal of Distance Education, 8*(1), 36–59.

Savery, J. (2003). *Application of "means of assistance" analysis to computer-mediated communication.* Unpublished manuscript, University of Akron.

Schrire, S. (2002). The learning processes, moderation and discourse patterns in asynchronous computer conferencing (Doctoral dissertation, Nova Southeastern University, 2002). *Dissertation Abstracts International, 63,* 2516.

Serwatka, J. A. (2002, April). Improving student performance in distance learning courses. *T.H.E. Journal, 29*(9), 46–63.

Shea-Schultz, H., & Fogarty, J. (2002). *Online learning today: Strategies that work.* San Francisco, CA: Berrett-Koehler.

Sherry, L. (2000). The nature and purpose of online conversations: A brief synthesis of current research. *International Journal of Educational Telecommunications, 6*(1), 19–52.

Smith, G., Ferguson, D., & Caris, M. (2001, April). Teaching college courses online versus face-to-face. *T.H.E. Journal, 28*(9), 18–22, 24, 26.

Teles, L. (2002, May/June). The use of web instructional tools by online instructors. *The Technology Source.* Retrieved September 29, 2004, from http://ts.mivu.org/default.asp?show=article&id=966

Theodore, P. (2001). Conclusions and recommendations. In P. Theodore, *The networked word: Toward a more complete description of the nature and educational utility of computer-mediated bulletin board discussions.* Retrieved September 29, 2004, from http://www.siue.edu/~ptheodo/chapter6.html

Van Rooij, S. (2000). Conflict management among adult learners in the computer-mediated environment. *WebNet Journal, 2*(4), 45–51.

Webster, J., & Hackley, P. (1997). Teaching effectiveness in technology-mediated distance learning. *Academy of Management Journal, 40*(6), 1282–1310.

Willis, L. (2002). The relationship among self-efficacy, instructor feedback, and technical support of learners in an online learning environment (Doctoral dissertation, University of Tennessee, 2002). *Dissertation Abstracts International, 63,* 1802.

Appendix 11A

The Relationship Between Goals, Types of Interaction, and CMC Tools

Goal	Synch./ Asynch.	Type of Interaction	CMC Tool
Establish an atmosphere of trust (Dabbagh, 2003)	A	Instructor-Learner	• Announcement page • Instructor information page
Build group coherence (Chism, n.d.; Serwatka, 2002)	A	Instructor-Learner Learner-Learner	• Instructor page • Student home page
Establish social presence (Baker, 2001; Gunawardena & Zittle, 1997; Rovai, 2002)	A	Instructor-Learner Learner-Learner	• Use emoticons and follow netiquette guidelines
Provide students with opportunities to interact with content in addition to the text:			
• External links (King, 1998)	A	Learner-Content	• External links
• Electronic case studies	A	Learner-Content	• Content modules
• Electronic online quizzes (Coates & Humphreys, 2001)	A	Learner-Content	• Online quizzes
Provide a permanent record for students to refer to	A	Learner-Content	• Archived chat • Online discussion
Provide students with procedural guidance on how to complete tasks (Martyn, 2003)	A	Learner-Content	• Electronic task aids • Electronic grading rubrics
Promote interaction and collaboration (time-sensitive issues/tutoring)	S	Instructor-Learner Learner-Learner	• Chat

Goal	Synch./Asynch.	Type of Interaction	CMC Tool
Group work (Cheng, Lehman, & Armstrong, 1991)	A	Instructor-Learner Learner-Learner	• Group tools
Individual means of assistance (Savery, 2003)	A	Instructor-Learner	• Email • Virtual office chat
Promote critical thinking, reflection, and cognitive learning (Dabbagh, 2003; Prammanee, 2003; Rossman, 1999; Schrire, 2002)	A	Instructor-Learner Learner-Learner Learner-Content	• Online threaded discussion • Electronic blackboard note-taking/journal area
Provide feedback to students (Chism, n.d.; Rossman, 1999)	A	Instructor-Learner	• Digital drop box
Develop and refine written communication skills (Chism, n.d.)	A	Learner-Learner	• Online threaded discussion—student moderate/summarize
Provide students with exposure to different perspectives and ways of solving problems (Alexander, 1995)	A	Instructor-Learner Learner-Learner	• Online threaded discussion
Bring in a content expert (Peters, 2000)	A	Instructor-Learner	• Online threaded discussion
Online tutoring (Chism, n.d.)	S	Instructor-Learner	• Chat
Provide technical help	A	Learner-Content	• Online manual/tutorial
Provide learner control / empowerment over the learning situation (Moore, 2002)	A	Learner-Content	• Online course modules, PowerPoint, multimedia

Goal	Synch./ Asynch.	Type of Interaction	CMC Tool
Formative assessment on student perceptions on course format (Martyn, 2003)	A	Instructor-Learner	• Online survey
Address diverse groups of students:	A	Instructor-Learner	
• Learning styles (Allen, Bourhis, Burrell, & Mabry, 2002)	A	Learner-Content	• Multimedia content in course content modules
• Gender issues (Kimbrough, 1999)	S	Instructor-Learner	• Chat tutorials
• Disabilities (Berge, 1995)	A	Instructor-Learner Learner-Learner	• Online threaded discussion
• Different personality types including shy or introverted students (Bailey & Wright, 2000; Bischoff, Bisconer, Kooker, & Woods, 1996; Gillette, 2001; Goldberg, 2000)	A	Instructor-Learner Learner-Learner	• Online threaded discussion
Learner satisfaction (DeBourgh, 1998; Drnek, 1998; Geary, 1998; Mowen & Parks, 1997)	A	Learner-Instructor	• Online threaded discussion

Part V

Adult Learning Includes Senior Learners

12

Meeting the Needs of Older Adult Learners: The Development of a Learning in Retirement Institute

Charlene L. Martin

Interest in older adult education is developing at an opportune time as the demographic composition of the United States is shifting from younger to older people for the first time in American history. This age wave is producing an increasing number of retirement-age people who are interested in participating in academic programs. As institutions of higher learning attempt to accommodate the educational interests of these older people, educators must seek to better understand who these learners are, what their motivations are, and how these programs can impact their lives.

The over-65 age group has grown more than twice as fast as the rest of the population in the last 20 years, and that growth is expected to increase with the aging of the baby boomers and the continued decline of birth rates. Projections indicate that by the year 2030, this age group will comprise over 21% of the total population—about 70 million Americans (U.S. Department of Health and Human Services, 1999). With continued improvements in lifestyles and medical technology, these retirement-age adults are also healthier, more active, and expected to live longer than previous generations.

Older adults are currently seeking to continue, renew, or begin their education in increasing numbers. Almost 19% were enrolled in formal learning experiences in 1999 (U.S. Department of Education, 2001b). As more seniors seek educational opportunities, the challenges for higher education involve changing institutional philosophies and practices. Resistance on the part of institutions of higher education to accommodate older learners would not be surprising. Education for the young clearly benefits society, whereas many might argue that educational programming for older people is not a sound investment—in part because their contribution to society may be perceived as diminished. This argument is based on negative stereotypes of older people and lacks recognition of the positive aspects of aging.

One way to discourage stereotyping is to study who these older learners are and why they are seeking to participate in educational programming. Williamson (1997) advocates this approach when he states, "We need to be thinking and planning now for this future and taking note of what those who have reached the Third Age have to tell us about our social and educational futures from the vantage points of their own lifelong learning" (p. 174).

This chapter reviews research on older adult learners and one model of older adult education, the Learning in Retirement Institute. I use the Worcester Institute for Senior Education at Assumption College as an example of such an institute and I explore the benefits to both the individual and to the college. Continuing educators who are considering the development of a Learning in Retirement Institute may draw from this model to achieve an understanding of the needs of older learners. They will also find valuable, practical information to assist with the start-up of such a program, and recommendations to facilitate the success of the program while avoiding possible pitfalls.

What We Know About Older Adult Education

Understanding older learners, their motivations, and the barriers that may prevent them from participation can provide planners with information critical to the development of programs that address their needs. It can also assist with rationales to support institutional policy concerning older adult education. The field of older adult education is relatively new, but a variety of models already exist. Those higher education institutions that do provide some type of programming for older adults typically offer Elderhostel courses, tuition-waiver programs, or Learning in Retirement Institutes.

Older Adult Learners

While older people are as diverse as any other category of people, research demonstrates that there is a "typical" older adult learner. The demographic profile of older adults participating in learning programs at institutions of higher education describes a white female with at least some college education, a middle to high income, who is in self-reported good health (Bynum & Seaman, 1993; Danner, Danner, & Kuder, 1993; Lamdin & Fugate, 1997; Puccio, 1995).

Since those who participate in formal older adult education tend to be economically secure, why do they choose to participate in an educational program when they have the means to fill their leisure time in a variety of ways? The literature suggests that motivations of older adult learners include desire for intellectual stimulation (Bynum & Seaman, 1993; Lamdin & Fugate, 1997), pursuit of an interest (Lamdin & Fugate, 1997), learning something useful (Bynum & Seaman, 1993; Puccio, 1995), love of learning (O'Connor, 1987; Scala, 1996), and social contact (Bynum & Seaman, 1993; Danner et al., 1993; Lamdin & Fugate, 1997). Despite the diverse motivations for older adult learners, those related to cognitive interest always prove to be the strongest motivator, followed by a desire for socialization.

Given the great diversity among older people, it is not unusual to learn that many different reasons are given for lack of participation. Studies have found that these include financial issues (Danner et al., 1993), lack of awareness and complexity of admissions (Peterson, 1981; Lamdin & Fugate, 1997), as well as health issues, transportation, time constraints, parking, location of classes, dislike of being out at night, insecurity in a learning environment, and lack of interest (Graney & Hays, 1976; Peterson, 1981; Bynum, Cooper, & Acuff, 1978; Scala, 1996). Health issues generally pertain to either the problems of the participants or of a family member who needs care.

History of Learning in Retirement Institutes

Our understanding of old age has evolved over the years as our public and institutional policies reflect these changes. Society's understanding of late-life development has moved beyond the linear life plan to one that includes education, leisure, and work at any or every time of life. Consequently, old age is now seen as a time for creativity, and not necessarily passivity. In order to accommodate this emerging view of seniors as capable of active participation and governance over their own lives, colleges and universities began to develop academic programs specifically aimed at seniors rather than mainstreaming them into existing courses. One such model of programming is the Learning in Retirement Institute (LRI).

The first LRI was the Institute for Retired Professionals sponsored by the New School for Social Research in 1962. It was during the 1990s that LRIs experienced phenomenal growth with more than 250 institutes established in the United States and Canada, serving over 64,000 older learners (Linnehan, 1997; Swindell & Thompson, 1995).

More research became available on LRI in the last decade. Fischer, Blazey, and Lipman (1992) edited a detailed book that describes this model and outlines the process for establishing an LRI at a college or university. Drawing on information gathered from many different LRIs, it examines program design, instructional leadership, academic standards, marketing, recruitment, retention, fee structures, budgets, bylaws, and host institution issues. A comprehensive survey of all active LRIs in the United States and Canada was conducted in 1997 by DeJoy. It quantifies and describes program characteristics and investigates possible relationships between the characteristics of LRIs and those of their host institutions. Several descriptive studies trace the development of the New School for Social Research's Institute for Retired Professionals (Hirsch, 1978), North Carolina State University's Encore Program (Glass, 1995), Eckerd College's Academy of Senior Professionals (Nussbaum, 1984) and the University of North Carolina at Asheville's College for Seniors (Manheimer & Snodgrass, 1993). These case studies demonstrate the success of the programs and provide useful information on the common features of LRIs, but more importantly, they illustrate the distinctive nature of such programs.

The Learning in Retirement Institute Model

LRIs are campus-based learning organizations for older adults sponsored by colleges or universities. People over the age of 60 join the organization by paying an annual membership fee and are considered members as long as they continue to pay dues. A key factor is that members develop and often teach the courses that are offered and they administer the institute themselves. This highlights the idea that older people are able to contribute and produce resources and not merely consume them.

In an LRI, any member may propose a study group on a topic of interest. As the group leader, he or she acts as a facilitator of the learning process while the group researches and shares knowledge of the topic. The college sponsor usually provides classrooms and meeting space, and in some cases, some administrative and clerical services. A university-appointed director may act as a liaison between the membership and the college. Although members are not technically students of the institution, a strong bond can develop whereby the college encourages the loyalty of LRI members by involving them in the college community.

Each LRI is unique, based on both the nature of the sponsoring institution and the members themselves. Admission eligibility varies from a specific minimum age to no age specification, and from no previous education requirement to interviews by member-led admissions committees that determine educational and professional background. Membership fees fluctuate from free to a $1000 initiation fee. Curriculum development can be highly elaborate, involving a proposal by a member or group, with submission to a curriculum committee for approval, while other LRIs allow anyone who wishes to lead a class to do so. In some LRIs only members lead classes, whereas in others only traditional faculty are invited to lead. Still others use a mix of member-led and outside professionals. Most have their own organizational structure with committees and executive boards, but there is no uniformity to their methods. Size of membership ranges from about 50 to over 2000 with many capping their enrollment at a certain optimal number. This quick overview reveals that LRIs are flexible and their policies may be modified to fit their members' needs.

Distinctions Between Learning in Retirement Institutes and Other Models of Older Adult Education

Colleges and universities offer different models of older adult education. LRIs are member-driven organizations as opposed to institution-driven models of learning such as Elderhostel or tuition-waiver programs (traditional college courses that are tuition-free for seniors). LRIs depart from the traditional mode of higher education where the institution determines and defines the course of study and the expert who teaches it.

Although Elderhostel is an extremely popular form of older adult education, offering hundreds of travel/study courses throughout the world, it differs from LRIs in that its students are participants rather than creators of the programs. Similarly, older adults attending traditional college courses participate in order to attain a degree or to enjoy the intergenerational experience, but they do not have the opportunity to teach a course or the flexibility of non-credit programming.

Tuition-waiver programs were legislated in the 1970s because it was believed that older learners would attend college if financial barriers were removed. However, research reveals that free tuition is a low motivating factor (Chelsvig & Timmermann, 1979, 1982). Although thousands of colleges offer tuition-free courses, participation rates remain low with less than 1% of all students enrolled in undergraduate credit programs over the age of 65 (U.S. Department of Education, 2001a). Since these programs are designed with the assumption that removing the financial barriers would increase senior enrollment, the results are disappointing.

Older learners who participate in LRIs, Elderhostel, or tuition-free college courses share the dual motivations of a desire to learn and to socialize, but LRI members soon learn that there are added benefits. Through active participation in the governing of the LRI and the peer teaching of courses, LRI members may also receive the benefits of personal growth, increased self-esteem, and a sense of contribution and empowerment that contributes to successful aging (Martin, 2003).

In order to provide some insight into the functioning of an LRI, one model program will be featured in the next section. This model will be used to examine curriculum development, the role of group leaders, membership recruitment and marketing, socialization, program/course evaluation, governance, and the role of the host college.

Worcester Institute for Senior Education

The Worcester Institute for Senior Education (WISE) began in January 1993 on the campus of Assumption College and has since grown from 100 to almost 500 members, all between the ages of 55 and 90. The only LRI in central Massachusetts, it is open to all seniors interested in learning.

Central Massachusetts has a larger older adult population than the national average. It is a community that is home to 15 institutions of higher education, many of which offer free tuition to citizens over the age of 65. Yet WISE, as an LRI, fulfills a need for many older adults who do not desire the traditional learning format of courses with homework, exams, and credits, or classrooms populated by younger students. WISE offers older adult learners the opportunity to contribute their wisdom and service in order to create and administer an educational program.

The primary objective of WISE is to provide a quality educational opportunity to older adults, based on peer learning and active participation. There are no age limits or educational requirements. More than 70 courses were offered during the 2003–2004 academic year and enrollments topped 1,200, with most members taking two or three courses during each of the four five-week sessions. Other benefits of membership include special events, domestic and international study/travel tours, and participation in college programs and events.

Members may take as many courses as they like during each of the four sessions offered during the fall and spring semesters. Recent courses have included American Civil War, Parents and Children in Shakespeare's Plays, Images of the City in American Literature, Goddard's Legacy in Space Exploration, Poetry of Religious Experience, Literature of Social Protest, Macchiavelli, Education for Democracy, Biodiversity in the Oceans, and Hemingway's Vision of War.

Members who share their expertise from past vocations, avocations, or from research teach about 30% of the curriculum. A curriculum committee works to develop a course schedule from suggestions from the membership, and if no member is able to teach a proposed course, the committee invites an Assumption College professor or an expert from one of the other local colleges to lead the course. WISE also utilizes the expertise of various Worcester cultural and educational organizations by inviting representatives to facilitate courses. Examples include Navigating the Net for Health Issues at the University of Massachusetts Medical School, Legal Issues by the Worcester County Bar Association, The Nature of Worcester at the Massachusetts Audubon Society, In Their Shirtsleeves: Worcester's Industrial History at the Worcester Historical Museum, Egyptian to Contemporary Art at the Worcester Art Museum, Cosmology at the Worcester Ecotarium, Introduction to Worcester Architecture by Preservation Worcester, and Worcester Women's History by the Worcester Women's History Committee. A small stipend is offered to nonmembers who lead a course.

The special events committee schedules activities in order to encourage socialization among members outside of the classroom. This is instrumental in developing WISE's wonderful sense of community and in stimulating conversations that lead to new program ideas. One event per month is scheduled, and attendance ranges from 25%–50% of the membership. A sample of events includes lectures and slide presentations, concerts, museum trips, and theatre productions. Topics of recent lectures range from Crime in the 21st Century to Reflections on the Foundation of Christian Education. Since no classes are scheduled during the summer months, members enjoy the Summer Brown Bag Series as a welcome opportunity to socialize and to listen to a lecture or a performance. Members also showcase their creative talents by presenting several art exhibits and concerts, all of which are open to the college community.

The idea of offering study/travel trips originated from members of WISE. After participating in a WISE course on India, class members persuaded the group leader to organize a trip to that country. Each subsequent trip has involved themes such as art, music, or literature. A WISE member organizes the tour and leads the group of 30–40 people along with a professor who has expertise in the featured theme. Since the first trip to India, WISE members have traveled to London, Italy, Vienna, China, Ireland, Russia, Prague, and Jerusalem. The trips are also open to college students, employees, and alumni. For those who prefer travel closer to home, the domestic travel committee organizes trips to places such as Baltimore's Peabody Institute and Philadelphia's museums.

The financial objective of the program is to meet all costs through membership dues. This objective has been met every year. Dues are $120 for a full year or, for those who flee the New England winters, $70 for a half year. A surplus balance of more than $10,000 is typical. Assumption College offers in-kind contributions of classroom and event space. WISE presents an annual scholarship to a continuing education student and scholarship money is available for potential WISE members who cannot afford the annual membership fee. WISE started a fund to generate money to furnish a dedicated classroom and office space upon availability.

WISE is committed to program assessment and conducts evaluations of each individual course. Annual focus groups stimulate discussion and solicit solutions to potential problems. Results are communicated to the general membership through quarterly newsletters. A comprehensive survey of the entire membership has been conducted twice in 10 years. The results of both surveys provided valuable information to the strategic planning committees involved in the ongoing administration of the organization. Over 70% of the membership responded to both surveys, and 90% of the respondents rated WISE as excellent, as the following comment from the 1998 survey indicates:

> It has been an intellectual joy to be a part of this Learning in
> Retirement Institute. This experience has provided great stim-
> ulation and satisfaction and has enriched my life. The desire
> to acquire knowledge is one of the best medicines, and hav-
> ing a sense of community and belonging at this stage in life
> is so rewarding.

Assumption College, as the host institution, received the same favor-
able response. Members appreciate the sense of community they find in
WISE and at Assumption College.

The success of WISE is demonstrated by the willingness of its members to contribute to their institute's administration. Members may choose
to serve as a group leader or to join one of the working committees: council (governing body), curriculum, special events, membership, newsletter,
and registration. Volunteer opportunities beyond group leader and committee work include serving as class assistants, registration assistants,
newsletter photographers and columnists, special projects coordinators,
and orientation leaders.

WISE has contributed to the development of the older adult education movement by hosting development workshops for the Elderhostel Institute Network (EIN), assisting with three regional EIN conferences, presenting workshops at several Association for Continuing Higher Education and EIN conferences, and assisting in the formation of five new institutes throughout New England. The self-produced WISE video has been
used by EIN at development workshops and conferences.

Although WISE is an example of a successful LRI that clearly satisfies
older adult learners' desire for continued learning, it may not be obvious
how the college benefits from sponsoring such a program. The following
section provides insight into the benefits to both partners.

Benefits of Learning in Retirement Institutes to the Institute and to the Institution

Assumption College is a small Roman Catholic, liberal arts college. It
has a strong commitment to lifelong learning reflected in its mission
statement that declares a desire to develop "a life of inquiry within a
community of learning." The college fully supports WISE as an example
of lifelong learning and the president, provost, and dean of the college

frequently address the membership and acknowledge the importance of the program.

Benefits to the Learning in Retirement Institute

WISE benefits from its partnership with Assumption College in several ways. Most importantly, it receives free use of space for classes, special events, and clerical work. Space needs can become a serious issue for LRIs when they rely on their host institution to fulfill this need. At a small institution such as Assumption College, space is often at a premium. Despite the recent addition of new classroom buildings on campus, WISE classrooms are assigned after the scheduling of daytime courses for the full-time undergraduate population. However, WISE and the college administration use creative measures to overcome this potential problem. WISE schedules all of its courses in the afternoon, a time when the college offers fewer undergraduate courses. In order to expand its course offerings beyond the one available classroom that accommodates two back-to-back courses, several WISE courses are offered off-site at various museums throughout the city. Courses are also offered at the Worcester Senior Center and at two retirement communities. Although the long-range goal is for a room of its own, there have been no major difficulties in offering a curriculum that meets the needs of the expanding membership.

Besides the donation of space for classrooms and events, the college offers the services of a college administrator to provide support and to act as a liaison. WISE pays a small stipend to a college secretary to assist with clerical support, database management, and handling inquiries from the general public. This use of college personnel assists with the smooth functioning of the institute within the larger institution.

Other benefits to WISE from its partnership with Assumption include the availability of campus services such as the print shop, post office, bookstore, media services, and food service; the use of office equipment and phones; insurance, security, and maintenance; availability of college faculty to lead courses or give lectures; an open invitation to all college cultural and social events; and use of the library and bus shuttle. The college receives 20% of WISE's operational expenses in return for some of these benefits.

Benefits to the Institution

College administrators contemplating the development of an older adult program on their campus may wonder what benefits such a program would bring to a college. The cooperative partnership between Assumption College and WISE provides examples of such benefits. First, it increases community recognition of the college. With five hundred satisfied WISE members, the college has ambassadors within the community who promote a positive image of the college. The WISE program also generates publicity through its activities and awards. The program was highlighted in a recent Worcester economic impact study, featured in a town meeting on the role of higher education and community, and acclaimed by U.S. Senator Edward Kennedy as a college program that contributes to older adults and to the Worcester community at large. The Institute and the College have been recognized by the Age Center of Worcester, the Worcester Senior Center, the Elderhostel Institute Network, and the Association for Continuing Higher Education and have been featured in numerous newspaper articles and radio and television interviews.

A second benefit impacts the college development efforts. WISE contributes annually to the Continuing Education Scholarship Fund, individual members donate to the College Annual Fund, and the study/travel international tours contribute to Continuing Education's budget.

Learning and research opportunities are a third benefit to the College. Members of WISE assist the College in a variety of ways and are a valuable resource. They provide a rich resource for undergraduate and faculty projects by volunteering as interview and survey participants for undergraduate students. They serve as guest speakers for history, sociology, and women's studies courses; they cosponsor campus lectures, intergenerational art exhibits, and social events with the student government association and the alumni association; they generate internship opportunities for gerontology students; they offer the study/travel tours to the college community; and they serve on college committees such as centennial planning and reaccreditation.

A final benefit to the College is gained through the visible presence of these older learners on campus. Their enthusiasm serves as a role model to younger students, faculty, and administrators. It is gratifying to view the excitement they develop as a result of their pure love of learning. Members of WISE truly embody the principles of lifelong learning that this liberal arts college attempts to instill in its younger students.

As the director of the WISE program for over ten years, I have had the pleasure of watching the program grow and expand. I have seen how participation in WISE adds to the lives of older people in unexpected ways. I have also seen how the college has welcomed these older learners into the academic community. The key to the partnership's success is that the relationship is less like a contractual arrangement and more like a marriage in which each partner contributes to its success.

Lessons Learned

Although the story of WISE and Assumption College is a successful one, problems arose over the last 10 years that were addressed and resolved by the members and the college staff. It is from these, and observation of pitfalls that other LRIs have encountered, that a short list of lessons learned is provided here. It is hoped that these lessons will help others as they develop their own LRI.

- Sign a memorandum of understanding between the LRI and the institution at the beginning of your collaboration.

- Create clear bylaws for the governance of the LRI.

- Evaluate the program through course evaluations, membership surveys, and focus groups, and do so on a regular basis.

- Maintain member profiles to learn who your members are and what talents they can contribute.

- Be vigilant about the need for adequate classroom space—be creative and have backup plans.

- Remember to give recognition to member volunteers, to group leaders, and to the college.

- Develop ties to the college through intergenerational classroom and social activities and through development initiatives.

- The role of director requires patience and the ability and willingness to relinquish control.

References

Bynum, J. E., Cooper, B. L., & Acuff, F. G. (1978). Retirement reorientation: Senior adult education. *Journal of Gerontology, 33,* 253–261.

Bynum, L. L., & Seaman, M. A. (1993). Motivations of third-age students in learning-in-retirement institutes. *Continuing Higher Education Review, 57,* 12–22.

Chelsvig, K. A., & Timmermann, S. (1979). Tuition policies of higher educational institutions and state government and the older learner. *Educational Gerontology, 4,* 147–159.

Chelsvig, K. A., & Timmermann, S. (1982). Support services for older adult tuition programs. *Educational Gerontology, 8*(3), 269–274.

Danner, D. D., Danner, F. W., & Kuder, L. C. (1993). Late-life learners at the university: The Donovan Scholars program at age twenty-five. *Educational Gerontology, 19,* 217–239.

DeJoy, J. K. (1997). *Survey report of institutes for learning in retirement: Program characteristics and sponsor institute relationships* (Tech. Rep. No. 1). Athens, GA: University of Georgia, Learning in Retirement at the Georgia Center for Continuing Education.

Fischer, R. B., Blazey, M. L., & Lipman, H. T. (Eds.). (1992). *Students of the third age: University/college programs for retired adults.* Westport, CT: Greenwood.

Glass, J. C., Jr. (1995). A university's multidimensional educational program for older adults: From conception to birth. *Educational Gerontology, 21,* 555–568.

Graney, M. J., & Hays, W. C. (1976). Senior students: Higher education after age 62. *Educational Gerontology, 1,* 343–359.

Hirsch, H. (1978). Higher education in retirement: The Institute for Retired Professionals. *International Aging and Human Development, 8,* 367–374.

Lamdin, L., & Fugate, M. (1997). *Elderlearning: New frontier in an aging society.* Phoenix, AZ: American Council on Education/Oryx Press.

Linnehan, M. (1997). *Institutes for learning in retirement: The distance traveled and the road ahead.* Unpublished manuscript, Elderhostel Institute Network.

Manheimer, R. J., & Snodgrass, D. (1993). New roles and norms for older adults through higher education. *Educational Gerontology, 19,* 585–595.

Martin, C. L. (2003). Learning in retirement institutes: The impact on the lives of older adults. *Journal of Continuing Higher Education, 51,* 2–11.

Nussbaum, L. L. (1984). The Academy of Senior Professionals at Eckerd College. In C. M. N. Mehrotra (Ed.), *New directions for teaching and learning: No. 19. Teaching and aging* (pp. 75–83). San Francisco, CA: Jossey-Bass.

O'Connor, D. M. (1987). Elders and higher education: Instrumental or expressive goals? *Educational Gerontology, 13,* 511–519.

Peterson, D. A. (1981). Participation in education by older people. *Educational Gerontology, 7,* 245–256.

Puccio, E. (1995). Developmental needs of older adults: Implications for community colleges. *Community College Journal of Research & Practice, 19,* 255–265.

Scala, M. A. (1996). Going back to school: Participation motives and experiences of older adults in an undergraduate classroom. *Educational Gerontology, 22,* 747–773.

Swindell, R., & Thompson, J. (1995). An international perspective on the university of the third age. *Educational Gerontology, 21,* 429–447.

U.S. Department of Education, National Center for Education Statistics. (2001a). *Fall enrollment, 1999.* Washington, DC: Author.

U.S. Department of Education, National Center for Education Statistics. (2001b). *National household education survey of 1999.* Washington, DC: Author.

U.S. Department of Health and Human Services, Administration on Aging. (1999). *A profile of older Americans: 2000.* Washington, DC: Author. Retrieved September 29, 2004, from http://research.aarp.org/general/profile_2000.pdf

Williamson, A. (1997, May/June). "You're never too old to learn!": Third-age perspectives on lifelong learning. *International Journal of Lifelong Learning, 16*(3), 173–184.

Index